STORIES OFF THE WALL

STORIES OFF THE WALL
JOHN ROSKELLEY

THE MOUNTAINEERS

Published by
The Mountaineers
1001 SW Klickitat Way,
Suite 201
Seattle, Washington 98134

© 1993 by John Roskelley

Cloth edition: first printing 1993. Paper edition: first printing 1998

Published simultaneously in Great Britain by Cordee, 3a DeMontfort Street, Leicester, England, LE1 7HD

Manufactured in the United States of America

Edited by Linda Gunnarson
Cover design by Elizabeth Watson
Book design and typography by The Mountaineers Books

All photographs by the author unless otherwise credited

Cover photograph: John Roskelley and Uli Biaho from 17,000 feet on Great Trango Tower. (Photo © Galen Rowell)

Library of Congress Cataloging in Publication Data

Roskelley, John
    Stories off the wall / John Roskelley
        p. cm.
    Includes index.
    ISBN 0-89886-349-X (cloth)
    ISBN 0-89886-609-X (paper)
    1. Roskelley, John.   2. Mountaineers—United States—Biography.
I. Title.
GV199.92.R67A3 1992
796.5'22'092—dc20   93-22667
[B]   CIP

To my mother, Violet May Roskelley,
who I suspect is the real Mary Poppins
and
to my father, Fenton Samuel Roskelley,
who shared with me his love of the wilderness

CONTENTS

John Roskelley on the summit of Denali, 1992. (Photo by Jim Wickwire)

INTRODUCTION

Mountain climbing is slowly nurtured within the heart and soul with each new climb, and stems as much from emotion as it does from desire. The quote often attributed to George Leigh Mallory, "Because it is there," is much too simple an explanation for something that drives us to risk it all just for the view at our feet.

Ask me why I climb after I plummet out of control eighty feet backwards and head first toward a granite ledge and my answer will reflect the tension of the moment. Believe me, it won't be "Because it's there." But catch me gazing over an endless horizon from the sun-baked windless summit of Mount Rainier on a fall day with good friends and "why" becomes an unforgettable emotion worth repeating. It's not easily explained to those people who see the world from an office desk or through the windshield of their car. Nor should it be. The answer is proportionate to the sweat and pain, difficulties overcome and risks accepted, that each of us have to work through to reach our goal. To experience the sport is the only way to answer the question.

I don't believe I intended to carry my early curiosity about mountaineering to the extreme that I have. At fourteen, after reading Lionel Terray's autobiography, *The Borders of the Impossible,* I wanted to experience the sport, but perhaps it was the lure of adventure on other continents, or the rapport under stress shared by Terray and his partner, Louis Lachenal, as much as the sport itself. If I had read *Moby Dick* instead, I would have run off and sailed the seven seas. It was that time in my life when the spirit runs wild and there's little distinction between fantasy and reality.

My dad, an outdoor sports writer, feared by every fish for his finesse with the rod and by pheasants for his deadly eye, finally realized the futility of resisting a teenager bent on climbing and made the first move. One fall afternoon he said, "I spoke with the Spokane Mountaineers today and you'll be old enough to start their class this coming spring."

And so it was that in March 1965, at sixteen years old, I found myself tying knots, jamming cracks, learning about weather, stuffing packs, and participating as an equal with people even older than my parents. It was a new, if not unusual, experience for a teenager who had reason to believe adults were another species, to have a real identity other than "kid." When I had participated in school sports I found the coaching to be impersonal and heavy-handed, but I continued to climb because I was treated with respect by grown-ups whom I grew to admire. For them, my best was always good enough.

I remember my first climb that year, Mount Rainier, a peak that in certain conditions can bring a triathlete to his knees. As a youngster I ran everywhere: to the store, to and from school, after deer, any time I was on my feet. It paid off on Mount Rainier. Dressed in blue jeans, cotton insulated underwear, my dad's hunting hand-me-downs, and rubber

Fenton Roskelley with John after a successful fishing trip, about 1960. (Photo by Fenton Roskelley)

boots, I made the ascent without trouble, despite wearing crampons on the sides of my feet because they wouldn't stay put on the slick rubber.

I recall a 1:00 A.M. start, the cold chill as I waited for the group to rope up and move, the leader's headlamp seeking a route through the gaping holes in the ice, the dead-calm silence broken only by the squeak of biting crampons, and a thick soupy mist that lay upon the mountain like a comforter. Hours later and thousands of feet higher, we reached the cloud's ceiling, an atmospheric demarcation so distinct it was like the surface of the sea. I stepped from a whiteout world of suppression and vertigo to an indigo blue sky, sunshine, and a forever longing to be above those clouds.

My problem with mountaineering was not walking uphill or freezing to death in my own sweat, it was patience. I had none. Being tied to others traveling at the speed of a glacier, with stops for everything from blowing their nose to fixing their pack, almost ended my climbing career. And, eventually it would have—if I hadn't met Chris Kopczynski.

Steaming along at the pace of a locomotive across the final plateau on Mount Shuksan late that summer, I felt the presence of another on my heels. Stymied for eleven hours while climbing with the Spokane Mountaineers group, the impatient youths in the group were finally given an okay by the leader to set their own pace to the summit. It was either that or outright mutiny.

Leaving the rest of the group to inch their way forward, I punched in the afterburner and ran for the top, fully expecting to sit on the summit alone for half an hour. But instead, right behind me was Kopczynski, another young climber who had taken the Spokane Mountaineers basic mountaineering course at the same time as I. We had both gravitated to opposite crowds while taking the course: me to a wild and crazy beer-drinking bunch who used climbing as an excuse to party, and Chris to a sober, athletic group who considered climbing an extension of their training for school sports.

As much as I hated to admit it, I needed this guy who was expensively outfitted like a Zermatt guide and sporting a crewcut only a Marine recruit could appreciate, if for no other reason than to keep from losing my mind climbing at the pace of a snail. Apparently he was thinking along the same lines. We tested each other's commitment to the sport on top of Shuksan by dreaming out loud, convinced within a short time we were really brothers in disguise. Chris and I shook hands, and swore then and there that we would climb together from then on.

Our bond was impatience. On the summit of Mount Shuksan began a climbing relationship that changed our lives, influenced mountaineering throughout the United States, and is still intact today. Similar to the bull-like Terray, and the spiderlike Lachenal, Chris and I formed a perfect team, blending speed with strength, precision with finesse. Most important, we developed strengths as a team we might not have reached as individuals, challenging ourselves to greater extremes, and continuing to play the game despite, at times, the slim chance of success.

Chris and I climbed at every opportunity, whether it was bouldering in Spokane in midwinter, mountaineering in the Canadian Rockies, or trying to free-climb an aid route on Chimney Rock in northern Idaho. Throughout our adventures, though, we considered ourselves mountaineers, a breed of climber able to leap tall mountains in a single bound, the decathloners of our sport. We trained and coached ourselves, hardening muscles with pull-ups, sit-ups, push-ups, and bouldering, and improving our endurance by running, biking, and always climbing higher and higher until, exhausted and sore, we would collapse in a heap on top of some peak with a new record, then laugh and plan the next adventure.

Through four years of studying geology at Washington State University, I spent my holidays in Yosemite Valley learning big wall techniques and improving my gymnastic rock skills. Speed demanded efficiency, and mountaineering throughout the Northwest had given me that gift. In the fall of 1971, another Northwest mountaineer, Mead Hargis, and I shot up what was then one of the world's most difficult big wall routes, the North American Wall, in two bivouacs. It was just one of many grade V's and VI's throughout the United States and Canada that year for me.

In January 1972, I married my wife Joyce, and all but quit climbing for more than a year. It was a difficult time for a geologist to find permanent employment, so I took part-time employment in and out of Spokane. Late one night the following January, before I left for my graveyard shift at a tire retreading plant, I received a call from Dr. Jim Morrissey, leader of the 1973 American Dhaulagiri Expedition.

"We've got a spot open on the team," Morrissey said. "Would you like to go?"

I wanted to ask him where Dhaulagiri was, but then I thought, What difference does it make to a guy making $2.40 an hour burning forearm flesh over hot steam molds? "When do we leave?" I asked.

"There isn't much time. We leave February 15th."

I had a month to quit my job, get a passport, take out a $1,500 loan for a plane ticket, and convince Joyce that this was the last time I would do something so foolish. I was through retreading tires forever that night, but I never convinced Joyce I would stay home for good and never will.

Dhaulagiri, the sixth-highest mountain in the world, was the first step for me in a life of adventure among the highest and most remote mountains on earth. After twenty Himalayan expeditions in twenty years, I still yearn for more, but perhaps now with a little less heart. As the years have passed, each lengthy departure from my family has bled another drop of enthusiasm from me, while injury and illness from those expeditions has chipped away at my ambition and determination. But the view from above and the sweat and tears it took to stand there, along with the Sherpas and Tibetans, Baltis and Indians, who were there to help, have made my trip through time a precious gift I won't forget.

My success in the Himalaya and elsewhere is more a function of who I was with than who I am. I provided enthusiasm, energy, and expertise to every expedition, but so did others. No one can stand on top of a mountain and say honestly, "I did it alone." There are always those who go before us and provide knowledge; there are Sherpas and Baltis and lowland porters who shoulder the burden of our laziness and still pray to their gods for our safe return; there are our wives and husbands, friends and family, who write us letters and hold down the fort while waiting patiently; and there are our teammates, strong and weak, good and not so good, who are determined to make our struggle their struggle. For all of them, the summit was reached.

Through the years I have set personal standards in climbing because I believe mountaineering, which is free of judges, umpires, and referees, still needs those who participate to use self-control and raise the standards of the sport. I have been fortunate to follow the lead set by my contemporaries, such as Yvon Chouinard, Royal Robbins, and Reinhold Messner, and, in doing so, define my own parameters within which I would climb. Sometimes these self-imposed rules curtailed my success, sometimes they evoked controversy, but since setting standards for myself and living them, I've not had a summit I haven't earned.

As a group, many climbers are still more concerned with individual accomplishment at any price than with setting standards of expertise for themselves that fit their goals. *How* you reach the top is far more important than getting there.

We must ask ourselves, Why go to the Himalaya in this day and age to climb the highest peaks on earth and eliminate their main challenge—altitude—by using bottled oxygen? Or, just how much of an achievement is it now to summit Everest or any Himalayan peak using Sherpas above base camp to do everything from carry loads and cook meals to put up tents? Do we climb to eliminate work by paying others to do it for us, or do we climb to challenge ourselves? Why is it masses of climbers in huge, environmentally insensitive expeditions drag the peaks down to their level, rather than rise to the challenge?

I encourage each of you embarking on adventures of your own to police your own actions, accept responsibility for your methods, and raise your standards to a level acceptable to your peers in today's sport. After all, mountaineering is a means to personal growth.

The stories that follow are personal vignettes of events or people that changed me, influenced me, or motivated me in some way. I think back on them as having instilled many of the values I have expressed here. Like Aesop's fables, my stories have morals, but unlike Aesop, I had to learn these the hard way. I hope that by reading them here, you won't have to do the same.

IT WOULD BE THE ONLY TIME IN MY LIFE MY CROTCH
DID SOMETHING OTHER THAN GET ME IN TROUBLE.

THE EAST FACE

The first fixed bolt, a hangerless and bent rusty
nubbin, was twenty feet straight up and to my left. I
spotted the half-inch of metal protruding from the wall
despite its oxidized camouflage on the orange-lichened
surface of sweeping granite. Upon closer inspection, I
noticed two, maybe three, more, equally spaced at
three-foot intervals above the first. Ed Cooper and
Dave Hiser, vertical pioneers of the iron age of the
1950s and the East Face first-ascent team of Idaho's
Chimney Rock, had removed the hangers. Even a
fifteen-cent hanger was gold to our predecessors.

I wanted the security the bolts provided, if for no
other reason than to bolster my failing courage, which

was really no courage at all, just a bluff young men must display in times of peril. The lead, a real neck bender, leaned out over our belay like an angry parent, and appeared long and unprotected. The bolts not only eliminated the need for me to struggle to place more protection, but they had a reputation of being "bombproof." And usually bolts are. But... I had flown eighty feet on one climb when a "bomber" bolt pulled out of its hole and my belayer had been fumbling with his camera instead of belaying. Luckily, I pulled up short of cratering into a ledge. All my belayer could say in explanation was "Oops."

The bolts would enable me to bypass a skin-eating seven-inch-wide overhanging crack that was too big to fist-jam and too small to get my body into. The crack was a classic off-width. Having thrashed and skidded mightily in cantankerous others of its kind, the scars on my elbows and knees, as well as in my mind, throbbed a painful warning not to be too bold.

"I'm coming back," I yelled to Chris Kopczynski. "I can see some bolts, but I need hangers."

My position at the sharp end of the rope was precarious. I was twenty stories off the first impact point. The wall leaned out like a drunk in a doorway. Gravity was pulling me back. My legs were spread-eagled between two small toe ledges while my fingers were crammed into a crack behind a four-inch ledge above my head. I could retrace my moves back to Chris. I was still fresh. But once committed to the upper crack, there would be little chance of retreat without a fall.

"I don't have them," Chris replied.

"They're in your pack," I yelled.

"I took them out at the bottom to save weight," he admitted guiltily.

I was not surprised. Disappointed, dejected, and scared, but not surprised. Chris had been subject to momentary lapses of foresight, and throughout our mini-adventures had provided some interesting, and occasionally amusing, incidents.

For instance, during the previous winter, Chris and I decided to make the first winter ascent of Chimney Rock. The Horton Ridge road from Priest Lake to the trail was belly-deep to a bull moose in snow.

Chris called a Priest Lake resort operator down the road for winter transport. An hour later I was straddling 440 cc's of thundering Scorpion Stinger snowmobile. Chris chose to "ski" behind the machine while I drove. He attached our climbing rope to the snowmobile, let out 150 feet of 9mm perlon line, and tied it around his waist with a bowline knot: the equivalent to tying yourself permanently to a Brahma bull. He wasn't about to let that snowmobile get away, but he wasn't about to escape either.

I gunned the engine and sped up the steep logging road. Chris leaned back and relaxed at the end of the rope, skiing the mild corners like the competition water-skier he was. As we came to the first hairpin turn, I stood up on the machine to carry momentum into the corner and felt an unusual surge of power. I punched the throttle to the handlebar. The noise was deafening.

Suddenly, I felt a yank on the machine and glanced back—just in time to see Chris in mid-flight, still tied to the rope, flying headfirst into the creek at twenty miles per hour. I took my hand off the throttle and the machine stopped within a few feet in the thick snow.

Chris had felt the rope go slack at the hairpin and he didn't need a great deal of imagination to know what was going to happen next. As he fumbled and pulled on the bowline, the rope snapped taut over the creek like a bullwhip at the end of its reach. He couldn't untie fast enough. I jumped off the machine and postholed through mushy snow back along the hairpin to where Chris had hurtled over the bank. He was face down, one arm elbow-deep in the creek, covered in logging slash and corn snow. Disturbing a grizzly bear over a fresh kill was safer than approaching Chris.

"I'm going to kill you, Roskelley!" he screamed. "Get me out of here!"

"Hang on, I'll get you out," I assured him.

"You're going to wish you never got on that snowmobile, you son-of-a-bitch," he yelled.

Self-preservation surfaced. I realized he was mad enough to do anything, but unable to get himself out of his predicament. His skis were hung up in the slash, he was upside down, and the snowmobile had him strung taut like a professional roping horse and a hog-tied calf. I bartered.

"I'll get you out if you promise to calm down," I offered.

He bellowed and roared in anger, but soon came to his senses. "All right," he agreed. "I won't kill you, but I'm going to break every bone in your body."

That sounded reasonable. I released his skis, untied the knot, pulled him from the creek, then ran like hell. He was uninjured and quick, but no match for my speed, which was all the faster to preserve life and limb. It was the last time Chris tied into a rope except to climb.

Chris is especially strong. He's an athlete and was a "first-stringer" in wrestling and baseball in high school. He trained hard, didn't smoke or drink, and ran around with the right crowd. Even in high school, his muscles were defined and toned.

Weights had done wonders for Chris's big-boned frame. Where fishnet underwear draped over my eighteen-year-old, small-boned, 133-pound body like a trawler's net over a tuna, it fit snugly on Chris and detailed his finely toned muscles. But I had him in one category. Even though my arms and legs were thin as fence rails, I had a large chest. Samson had his hair, I had my chest.

Chris changed my life. I was headed for trouble before I discovered mountaineering. Petty things to be sure: fights, pranks, joyriding, even drinking. Enough so that my name and reputation were passed through the teachers' grapevine from junior high to high school long before I got there.

When Chris and I met in the spring of 1965, during the Spokane Mountaineers basic school, we were instant competitors. It wasn't until midsummer, while standing on the summit of Mount Shuksan waiting for the other Spokane Mountaineers to arrive, that we called a truce and joined together as a team.

I immediately took a liking to him. He was positive, excelled at sports, an archetypical "Polish" character full of pantomimes and ad-libs.

I liked to get things done quickly, and Chris had the same impatience. So what if his athletic-style crewcut made him look like a nerd and he seemed to be off in the clouds at times?

Chris and I learned technical rock climbing through trial and error. Mostly error. The Spokane Mountaineers basic school was a mountaineering course. We were mountaineers. In fact, on Chimney Rock, I was wearing mountain boots, corduroy knickers, and Norwegian insulated fishnet underwear.

The intensity and energy of a thundercloud was boxed up inside me, straining to burst forth. I dreamed of exploding through linebackers or lifting small cars, but I felt trapped in an undersized body. Climbing enabled me to use my mental intensity and physical size to an advantage. I could finally release my energy in a positive form. The East Face of Chimney Rock was just the beginning of a long storm that needed a release.

It briefly occurred to me that leaving the bolt hangers at the bottom of the climb was Chris's revenge for the snowmobile incident. We both knew from reading about the first ascent that Cooper had placed bolts. That's why we had brought the bolt kit, or so I thought. No, Chris wanted the second ascent of the route as much as I did. Customarily, the hangers were left in place. This was simply bad luck.

"I'm going for it," I said. "Get a good belay."

I traversed left toward the only crack system that broke the sweep of granite. Thirty feet from Chris, I found a mangled three-quarter-inch ring angle welded into the crack behind my four-inch ledge. I clipped a single carabiner to the ring and snapped the rope through. I was safe for the moment.

Blocks of granite and small cracks led straight up. Within minutes, I was forty feet higher and at the beginning of the seven-inch off-width crack.

I hate off-width cracks. Off-widths require a specialized technique I call "thrashing," which is very similar to removing the bark off a tree at a sawmill. Your flesh is removed cleanly at the knees and elbows by slipping along crystals between two narrow walls of rock. Ten feet of elevation gained in an off-width is equivalent to an inch of skin lost. I'm not a good thrasher.

My alternative was to shinny up the outside of the fifty-foot flake that formed the left wall of the off-width. From my view it looked more practical. I didn't think I could get inside the crack with my large chest.

The flake was as sharp as a dull axe and, like an axe, thickened slowly farther away from its edge. It would be six inches thick at my knees. The guillotinelike flake leaned slightly toward the valley floor. I figured I could eventually move from the flake into the wider upper crack—if I got that far.

If I didn't, it wouldn't make much difference. A potential 90- to 180-foot fall from somewhere off the flake on our old 9mm perlon rope would break the rusty iron ring-angle piton and jerk Chris off the ledge. He wasn't anchored. Anchoring the belayer wasn't part of the Spokane Mountaineers basic course in 1965.

The rope drag—friction on the rope as it passed through a carabiner attached to the old ring-angle and down to Chris—threatened to pull me off. It was like adding forty pounds to my waist. It just wasn't my day. In fact, the weekend hadn't started out so hot either.

Chris and I had left our laborer jobs working on Sun Mountain Lodge and Dude Ranch near Winthrop, Washington, at "beer-thirty," or quitting time. The afternoon was a scorcher. Even the rattlesnakes were panting.

Chris had slowed down my 1961 Ford Falcon as we entered Creston, a small blip on the road with a population of thirty-six and a speed limit of thirty-five. Two high school girls were crossing the road headed toward the Copenhaven Restaurant. I harassed them from the car as we drove by.

Fifteen miles past Creston a sheriff's car, red and blue lights flashing, screamed past us in a hurry toward Creston.

"I wonder what's going on?" I remarked. "We didn't see any accidents."

Chris had his eyes on the rearview mirror. They got bigger and his face flushed. I looked back. The sheriff had just completed a skidding, 180-degree turn. With lights and sirens blazing, he caught up.

Chris stopped the Falcon alongside the road. The officer got out of his car, put a large, white Stetson on his head, and approached the driver's side.

"What's the trouble, officer?" Chris asked.

"Plenty," he drawled. "You boys are under arrest."

"What for?" I asked.

The deputy was tall, maybe six-foot-two or -three. He was intimidating, especially with the Stetson cocked forward and a big .357 Smith on his hip. He leaned into the driver's side window to get a better look at me. I felt as though he had just caught me violating his daughter.

"You did it," he growled.

"Did what?" I asked.

"You know what," he said, as if it would burn his tongue if he said it.

It was a typical teenage stunt. I was caught. The "crime" would have received a few laughs in Spokane, but Creston was redneck country. Wheat farmers, homesteaders, and cattle ranchers resided generation after generation in these parts.

Then the bad news. The Lincoln County judge was a long-time resident of Creston. With a population of only thirty-six, one of the girls could have been a relative of his. Who knows. I was out fifty bucks for vagrancy and we hadn't even got to the climb.

But that was yesterday, and fifty bucks was a lot easier to come up with than the strength needed to climb the flake.

"Hey, man," Chris hollered up to me as I surveyed the flake, "let's come back tomorrow with the hangers."

I liked the idea. In fact, I really didn't want to be there. But I was committed. First, I didn't think I could retrace the last forty feet. Second, I was still young and stupid. Death happened to others.

I started up the flake shinnying like I was climbing a fifty-foot piece of three-quarter-inch plywood by its edge: hands with knuckles to my face and thumbs down; knees and crotch squeezed tight. Ten feet up I knew I had made a mistake.

There was no retreat. I either reached the top or the name Roskelley would go down in Webster's meaning "stupid stunt." The rope drag was pulling me off, the flake was greasy, mostly smooth, and I was sweating like a dripping faucet. I slowly dug a groove in my chest as I inched upward using every bit of friction from my body on the rock. My throat was parched.

The cool air inside the chimney next to me was inviting, but impossible to reach. A rock lizard, clinging effortlessly to the vertical wall of the chimney, hesitated, then dashed into the darkness and coolness of the crack.

Chris sensed impending disaster. Never in our two years of climbing had he heard me wheeze and struggle that hard before.

I made another ten feet. My forearms were pumped with blood from my hands squeezing the flake. They looked like turkey legs. I wasn't going to make it.

I glanced at Chris for the first time since starting up the flake to see if he was ready for my plunge. He was sitting on the ledge, shirt sleeves pulled down over his hands, looking between his legs, shaking his head. It was a "no confidence" vote if I'd ever seen one.

That was all I needed to fight another ten feet up the flake. But it wasn't enough. I was too weak. My hands were going numb and my inner thigh muscles, weak from squeezing, were losing their grip. I started to slide to my death.

The heavy corduroy in the crotch of my pants saved my life.

As I prepared to scream and take the plunge, I slid onto a one-inch chip on the edge of the flake. The bottom portion of my knickers' crotch zipper caught enough for me to regain some strength. Not enough to climb, but enough to hold on for a few minutes more. It would be the only time in my life my crotch did something other than get me in trouble.

Until then, I could not let go with my hands except to slide them upward. To my left and within reach was a thin horizontal crack. Desperately, I gripped the flake with my right hand, reached behind me and to my right side with my left, and unhooked a baby angle piton from my hardware sling. All my concentration was in focusing my remaining energy into hanging on despite total fatigue.

I placed the angle in the crack and hit it once with my hammer. It was all I could do. I put a carabiner and a nylon aid sling on the piton, gripped the sling, and jumped. The pin held.

I finished the second pitch and the climb that day. We climbed the East Face in three and a half hours. The first ascent had taken two days. Members of the Spokane Mountaineers, who considered us a bit crazy before the climb, were now, more than ever, convinced we would not get much older.

Scars leave a lasting impression on your skin and your memory. Have you ever forgotten how you got the scar on your knee as a child, or the one on your shoulder?

The flake left a scar on my mind. It changed my life. Death was a reality. It no longer was something that could happen only to someone else. I felt Death over my shoulder as I clung to that flake, and I didn't want to feel it again.

My climbs became bolder in later years and took on new dimensions, but since the flake, I calculate my chances much more carefully. Our climb of the East Face of Idaho's Chimney Rock is why I'm alive today.

STILL FIGHTING FOR AIR, YOU LOOKED AT ME WITH
YOUR ONE GOOD EYE AND ONE BAD EYE AND SAID,
"GAWWD, ROSKELLEY! YOU'RE NOT THE
CLASSLESS BASTARD I THOUGHT YOU WERE."

A LETTER TO AN OLD FRIEND

Dear Bob:

Digging through my old climbing gear yesterday, I backed up into a corner of boxes and was stabbed in the ass. Guess what? It was the Chouinard Thrutch/ Crutch you gave to me for my twenty-fourth surprise birthday party. Concrete proof that climbers should not be allowed spare time to think.

I have to admit it was in better taste than the black doll-sized coffin, complete with red rose and death certificate, I built and presented to you on your fortieth birthday. But, as you now know, my gift was practical. Forty is the end.

Chouinard, with all his experience in climbing techniques and tool development, couldn't have come up with a more versatile tool for climbers than the Thrutch/Crutch. Adding a cardboard adze and pick head to the armpit pad of an old crutch increased its performance for me, a self-proclaimed mountaineer, and the nail, in place of a ferrule or a crutch's rubber slip pad, gave it the security found only in a Pilot USA. What a great gift idea for a guy still recovering from toe amputations after Dhaulagiri!

And talk about marketing. I always wanted to send the "hang tag" you wrote and attached to the crutch to Chouinard for his catalog:

CONGRATULATIONS ON YOUR NEW
CHOUINARD THRUTCH/CRUTCH
FOR AGING AND INFIRM CLIMBERS

When you're thrutchin' and a'puffin'
Hangin' out on that big wall,
Perhaps this Chouinard Thrutch/Crutch
Will save you from a fall.

'Cause while the years have been good to you
We notice with chagrin,
That those once strong knees have acquired a bend
And there's a sag to that once proud chin.

Therefore, we hope this brand new climbing tool
Will help you keep your cool,
So your name will go down in history
With Harlin, Terray, and Buhl!

Happy 24th, Bibs,
Bob

I always wanted to know why you chose those particular deceased climbers for me to join in history? I think Cassin, Robbins, and Bonington, who are still around hassling the alpine clubs, would have been more appropriate.

Can you believe it's been more than seventeen years since that party? We played the game well in those early years, Bob. There were more than a few "death certificates" ready to be signed by the Big Coroner, but for some reason the pen got lost. If you ask me, we had Him laughing so hard, He never got around to it.

We made a great team in the mid-sixties and early seventies. You may not have thought so at times, having to drag a kid ten years your junior around, but you changed my life and gave me some direction. Believe it or not, you were my hero: you had graduated from college, traveled through Europe, were working as an advertising executive for that big sign corporation, and, most important, remained single and dated great-looking gals at the ripe age of twenty-six. That was impressive to a sixteen-year-old.

Do you remember our first fiasco? Let me remind you. It was in the Grand Tetons in 1965, our first year of climbing. You and I, along with another young neophyte, Jim Mhyre, attempted the South Face of Symmetry Spire. We were cocky as hell after a successful climb of Mount Moran's CMC route several days earlier. There wasn't a route that was too tough or a peak too high after that climb.

If one of the three of us on the climb knew what an anchor was, he wasn't telling. And runners? They were the nerds in school back then, who ran cross-country. The Spokane Mountaineers 1965 climbing school taught the basics: bowline on a coil, sitting belay, and the nut-crunching shoulder/dulfersitz technique needed to climb Mount Rainier, Mount Shuksan, or Mount Moran. There was none of that "daredevil" stuff rock climbers were into. Come to think of it, A. F. Mummery, in 1879, had equipment as good as and better knowledge of technique than we did. And you know what they say about a little knowledge.

I knew we were short some neurons when we started up Symmetry's wall with three pitons, a couple of locking steel carabiners, one piton hammer, a softball-sized rock (just in case the pitons had to come out), an old Goldline rope, and no idea if or where there was a route. But what we didn't know wouldn't kill us, right?

We had reputations at stake. Reputations that had taken a whole spring to develop. We were known by some of the old-timers as "kamikazes," "the suicide squad," even as "idiots," but I think these were just affectionate euphemisms. Well, maybe not always.

As the Spokane Mountaineers hiking group followed the trail to the summit, we broke off below the South Face and, with me in the lead, boldly began to climb an obvious crack system. Of course, within a few short seventy-five-foot pitches, I was in over my head, leading difficult cracks and surmounting small overhanging roofs without protection.

As we angled up and left over blank granite and large roofs, retreat by rappeling became impossible. We didn't have the gear to do it safely anyway. Down-climbing the route was out of the question. I don't know about you, but this was the first time that climbing really scared me. We may not have talked about it on the face, but we either had to climb out of our mess, be rescued, or die—and even back then, there was no way I was going to be rescued.

We got lucky late that afternoon. After traversing the entire face and climbing a thousand vertical feet, we escaped with one rappel into the South Couloir. If I hadn't been stuck in the Tetons for the rest of the week with the Spokane Mountaineers, I would have gone home and never set foot on rock again.

But in those early days, I was short on brains and long on dreams. Originally, I counted on mountain climbing as a way for me to escape the pressures of youth, and an opportunity to burn up some energy without getting into trouble at home or at school. Many of the older Spokane Mountaineers, our mentors, such as Pete Van Gelder, Joe Collins, Bill Boulton, Will Murry, Bill Fix, and others, treated me like an adult. Imagine that! That was magic to me at sixteen. Their acceptance of me as an equal was the single most important reason why I continued to climb and strive to be the best. I'll never forget Bill Fix's write-up on our climb of Mount Moran in the Autumn 1965 issue of the Spokane

John Roskelley leading an exposed traverse on the North Peak of Index, Washington Cascades, 1967. (Photo by Chris Kopczynski)

Mountaineers' journal, *The Kinnikinnick*. The last paragraph read, "A special commendation is due John Roskelley for his help in route finding and leading to the summit from Drizzlepuss. At sixteen, he has to be dubbed 'most promising new climber.'" That one statement sent me off on a career that hasn't stopped in twenty-seven years.

If there was one peak that I felt taught us humility, it was the North Peak of Index. Chris Kopczynski and I tried it twice, but were rained out or lost the route both times. You joined us for our third attempt, in 1967, but again, the coastal rain washed our attempt down the valley. Finally, you and I succeeded on my fourth attempt that same year.

It wasn't easy. Following the guidebook's description, instead of our noses, was like trying to read someone else's mind. Where does "Ascend left sharply and then angle right up slabby rock to the crest on the left" lead? Just as bad was "Continue to traverse across an exposed slab with a fifteen-foot section of fingertip holds to the base of a steep brushy gully." There were dozens of exposed slabs, fingertip holds, and brushy gullies, but the description was typical of guidebooks.

After a full day of slabs, vertical brush pitches, and confusion, we summited as that gray, thick, coastal mist enveloped the Index peaks. Just when I thought we'd stolen the summit clean and would escape without a problem, Index snagged our rope on the descent as I tried to retrieve it after a rappel, then dumped an ocean of rain upon us. As you spread your vapor cloud–thin sheet of dry cleaner's plastic over us while we perched on the slimy, wet rock below our stuck rope, I echoed your disparaging thoughts. It looked like the beginning of a nasty bivy. But....

I rummaged around in my pack, unintentionally pulling the plastic off both of us. "Dammit Roskelley," you said, jerking your share back over your legs, "what are you doing?"

I had a secret. I kept searching for the one thing I knew would make your day and ease the pain of a wet, skin-wrinkling bivouac. I found it at the bottom of my pack. With an explosion that I thought might have been heard clear into Seattle, I popped the pop-top off a cold Rainier beer.

"OH, GAWWWD! That's greeaaat! Great!" Then you laughed your breathless, gasping laugh that always ended in a coughing, close-to-death fit. Still fighting for air, you looked at me with your one good eye and one bad eye and said, "Gawwd, Roskelley! You're not the classless bastard I thought you were."

That made *my* day, too.

Then there was our 1969 first ascent of the North Face on Lions Head in northern Idaho, an eight-hundred-foot-high wall on a mountain of granite, painted in black and ocher-colored lichens, and protected from climbers by its remoteness. Within Yosemite Valley, Bob, that climb would have been an instant classic, but hidden in remote northern Idaho, with a three-hour hike up and over two major ridges and through some of the worst slide alder and devil's club in the Selkirk range, it was still unclimbed and even unattempted.

Despite starting late in the afternoon, we free-climbed and aided three long pitches to a wide, comfortable ledge. It was a classic bivy site on a granite ledge made just for bivouacs. Radiant Indian-summer heat kept us warm into the night, until an early September frost crept through the valley below, chilling the morning air and laying a fine coat of ice crystals on the moist lichen. It was our excuse to sleep in and watch deep shadows give way to tamarack yellows, huckleberry-bush reds, and the iridescent greens of sunlit creek bottoms. Would our lives have been poorer not to have experienced that sunrise halfway up the North Face? I think so. I can sit here today and recapture that scene in my mind as it happened, smell the evergreens and sweet huckleberries, hear the moose grunting for her calf, and see the swirl of insects rise above the creek. Nature's serenity and peace overwhelmed us both.

By noon, we had enjoyed three more pitches of free-climbing, with an occasional piton for aid. A short pitch of pull-ups over blocks put us on the summit ridge, which we walked to the top.

Recently, Bob, a young climber walked up to me in a climbing store and said, "My partner and I free-climbed your route on the North Face of Lions Head in a day."

But, Bob, it took twenty-three years for someone just to repeat it, let alone improve on it. I think that speaks highly for our determination in those days.

I still think back on our ascent of Mount Robson as one of our best, though. It wasn't so much a climb as an "event." We weren't alone on this one—in the beginning. With Pres Ellsworth and Mike Quigley making up one two-man team and us the other, we were able to separate and still climb the peak.

Do you remember lifting Ellsworth's pack at the trailhead? Surprised, you said, "This thing seems awful light, Pres. What are you taking for food?"

"Just these," he said. And out of his shirt pocket came a pair of well-used pink panties fresh off that college gal he said good-bye to in Spokane.

Then Quigley asked him if he was going to share. That set the tone for the weekend.

There wasn't much nutrition in those panties. Halfway to our intended camp on the SSW Arete route, both he and Quigley tired, then bivouacked just above treeline. We, of course, reached high camp, a rock shelf that had once held a wood floored fiberglass hut flown in via chopper by the Canadian Park Service. We had found pieces of yellow fiberglass on the route up and knew an avalanche had destroyed at least that portion the previous winter. But the wood floor, still in place, made a great platform where we could set up our plastic sheeting as a makeshift shelter.

Contrary to Ellsworth's and Quigley's belief, I did feel a smidgin of remorse at our high camp, a thousand feet below Little Robson, when they didn't show that night. But not so guilty that we didn't enjoy Quigley's bottle of fine red wine, part of the weight I offered to carry for him to high camp, as his exhaustion set in and Pres slowed to a crawl.

The following morning was a summit day just meant for Team

John Roskelley on the Schwarz Ledges, Mount Robson,
Canadian Rockies, 1968. (Photo by Bob Christianson)

Christianson/Roskelley. As we inched our way through the limestone cliffs and shale bands below Little Robson, Mount Robson's lower subpeak, two men descended toward us. It was Hans Schwarz, the famous Austrian guide, pioneer of the route and namesake of the difficult traversing ledges that crossed beneath the massive icefall overhanging the Great Couloir. He and his client were descending without success.

"Zee Schwarz Ledges are bad. Very bad," he warned us. "We could not cross."

I had the feeling he wanted us to save time and descend right there. But we had to see for ourselves. He was right. The ledges were no longer visible beneath the rock-hard blue ice plastered in the couloir. But youth and inexperience have their advantages. Without a second thought, or perhaps even a first, I led horizontally across with my 95cm Stubai in one hand and a twelve-inch ice piton in the other. It would have been a lot easier if the several frontpoints on my old Austrian crampons hadn't bent and curled under my boots. But that taught me what I had already guessed from reading Lionel Terray's book, *The Borders of the Impossible*. Equipment is no substitute for skill. I think we even surprised ourselves.

Reaching the summit of Mount Robson under clear, windless skies, punctuated with Christianson wit, was one of my favorite moments in the mountain world. But Mount Robson, that mountain of trouble, didn't let us escape without an argument.

Ellsworth and Quigley, anxious to get a head start for the summit the next morning, passed through our bivouac camp, planning to sleep on top of Little Robson that night. It wasn't a good idea. The stifling afternoon heat set the stage, and soon the villains arrived, an army of cumulonimbus, boiling and seething across the Canadian Rockies. Horizontal squalls of rain and wind buffeted our cramped bivy plastic as bolts of lightning exploded, first above us, then upon us.

Our teammates bolted down from Little Robson, chased by squalls of rain and snow, then burst into our camp, as if safety lay in numbers. It didn't. Lightning flashed nearby, exposing the fear in our faces, followed furiously by bursts of thunder that shook the rock outcrop where we were perched. The four of us squatted inside the plastic on our foam mats, expecting to be Kentucky Fried by sunrise.

There was silence within our feeble shelter during the storm—a silence known only to those expecting to die, as if each of us wanted to use the time left to examine the meaning of his life. Talk wouldn't have helped.

When the violence of the storm did pass, it left only the soft, soothing touch of steady rain upon the plastic. Our hair resumed its natural laid-down position, and the metal tent poles ceased to whisper death in our ears. After anxious and relieved chatter, we fell asleep, curled tightly, puppy-style, within the confined space, exhausted from the tension of death. The storm left to pursue the heat lying over the plains of eastern Alberta.

Well, Bob, as you wrote on the Thrutch/Crutch, the years have been good to us, and, most likely, they will continue to be so. I've climbed a lot of peaks since our escapades, some of the great climbs of the world. But, you know, I wouldn't take one of them in place of the memories we earned together.

The difference between then and now lies in the purpose. Climbing was fun with you, Bob, a sport to enjoy, create a little hell, and maybe, just maybe, climb a peak. But as climbing became more of my life, it grew into a task, an assignment of sorts, to justify corporate money, months of time, and, of course, to stroke my own ego. I have to say, I miss the innocent adventures of youth.

I'm looking forward to our next trip, Bob. I can't promise you it will be peaceful. My kids will see to that. By the way, your greatest "summit" was marrying Carol, and, despite "keeping your cool," like Harlin, Terray, and Buhl, you're still on my list of heroes.

See you at Christmas!

John

'YOU'RE GOING TO LOSE THAT ARM,' SOMEONE SAID IN
THE DARKNESS.

UNDERGROUND

KOP Construction out of Spokane, Washington, bid on commercial jobs throughout the Pacific Northwest. Motels, marinas, small businesses, just about anything with potential to come out ahead was KOP's specialty. The company was always in need of good laborers.

During the summer season of 1968, Chris Kopczynski, the owner's oldest son, and I would no sooner settle into an apartment or room in one town when a strike or fire danger would shut the job down. Kop, as Chris's dad was known, would then call around to his foremen to see who would take a couple of hard-working laborers. Although we were just college students working summers, Chris and I were considered the best KOP hired. We prided ourselves in giving nine hours' hard labor for eight hours' pay. We always had jobs.

A laborer is part beaver, part badger, but always low man on the totem pole. As in any job, though, you can learn from it. I learned to anticipate my next assignment, get it done quickly, then move on. The foremen seldom had to spend time telling me what to do.

It was simple. Ninety percent of the work seemed to be repairing, redoing, or patching some carpenter's, steelworker's, or plumber's mistakes.

"Roskelley," some foreman would yell, "some idiot built this retaining wall in the wrong spot. Get a sledgehammer and knock it down. Then see the plumber. He's got a cement floor to remove. Somebody poured it before he was supposed to."

It was never "I built this retaining wall in the wrong spot" or "I poured the wrong floor." It was always an "idiot" or "somebody" else who screwed up. By the time I quit work as a laborer, I figured everyone I worked with in construction must have been either retarded or born without a name.

Chris and I were without a job once again in August 1968. We had finished a real estate building in Twisp, Washington, and a marina on Priest Lake in northern Idaho. In short, we had hustled ourselves clean out of work.

Then Kop received word that his foreman at the Pend Oreille Mine needed a couple of good laborers. KOP was general contractor for building a conveyor belt system to remove ore from the depths of the mine. Our job would be to carry steel bars and I-beams for the steelworkers, drill holes in the walls of the tunnels, and take care of general cleanup. The job sounded like an adventure, so we eagerly accepted the work. Besides, we would get per diem pay and hazard pay. Mine work was dangerous.

The Pend Oreille Mine, located in the remote northeastern corner of Washington, a few miles from British Columbia and Idaho, was a lead and zinc producer and the deepest mine in the state. Black bears, mule deer, elk, Rocky Mountain bighorn sheep, and Woodland caribou were just a few of the big game animals that thrived in the dense forests and thick underbrush. Sasquatch, better known as Bigfoot, was reportedly spotted frequently late on Saturday nights and was believed to inhabit the area. The local beer distributor was also a wealthy man.

People, mostly hippies and transients, had disappeared around Metaline Falls, the small mining town a few miles south of the mine. This was right-wing country. Far right. Almost off the page. Miners, loggers, and cement plant workers took their privacy, their right to hunt, and their free time seriously. Long-hairs didn't walk into the only two taverns in town, and "dope" was something they called their kids. Chris and I, conservative and construction workers to boot, fit right in.

My 1961 Ford Falcon, always thirsty for another quart of oil, had been driven too many miles up mountain roads and was too sick to leave home. I rode from Spokane to Metaline Falls with Larry Rupp. Chris would arrive a week later.

Rupp, a World War II vet and twenty-five years our senior, was a professional laborer. He made himself indispensable on every job, hustling here, fixing this, moving that. Rupp could run and repair anything that was man-made. We had worked together all summer the year before building a dude ranch in the North Cascades.

I had a lot of respect for Rupp. Despite being an older man in a young man's job, Rupp could work us college kids into a heap because he was in excellent health and, more important, had construction savvy. He knew the type of tricks only an old dog would know, like when to bust his butt and when to lean on the shovel. Rupp didn't smoke, and didn't drink more than a few beers. He had an extensive Marine vocabulary that, when used, seemed a natural part of the explanation or conversation, not a prerequisite for manhood. But he sure told some great jokes. Chris and I learned a lot from Rupp.

As the newest crew member, I was treated like any "new kid on the block." When I walked into the miners' room with Rupp at three o'clock in the morning, I was greeted with silence and suspicion by some burly guys. There were more fight scars on their faces than on a group of silver-tipped grizzlies at a salmon spawning ground. They quickly went back to putting on their coveralls and checking out their headlamps. Clean, dry, reliable equipment reduced injury and death in an occupation with the second-highest rate of industrial accidents. Our shift was early. We were construction workers, not miners. Our job was to build the new conveyor belt system from the ore crusher at the lowest level of the mine to the surface entrance. Like most mines, the Pend Oreille worked on a "skip" method of removing the ore, which was transported to a shaft that rose steeply to the surface. The "skip," or ore cart, was loaded and winched at a high rate of speed to the surface on a set of railroadlike tracks. But this system was too antiquated and slow. The conveyor belt was being installed at an expense of millions of dollars to increase profitability as the market price of ore fell.

The miners worked in three shifts to keep the mine continually in production. We worked our eight hours and were out of the mine by eleven o'clock in the morning, because at eleven, the miners blasted the tunnels. After the smoke and dust cleared, they went back in to scoop up the ore, transport it to the skip, and winch it to the surface for processing.

Rupp introduced me to the foreman, John Clark, who was as old as a Galapagos tortoise. He was somewhere between seventy and ninety. I don't think he knew. John was about my height, five-ten, and weight, 150 pounds, and had hands the size of ham hocks. His hands were so big it seemed like they belonged to someone else twice his size. The skin on his face reminded me of old, worn saddle leather, and his eyes were a dull cobalt blue, as if he had already died. We hadn't even started work yet, and John was greasy and dirty. He was looking me over good. Then he spoke.

"What the hell did they send me now?" He wasn't thrilled. "Whatta I gotta do to get some decent help down here? What's ya name, boy?"

"John Ros..."

"Shut up and listen carefully," he broke in. "You ever worked an air drill? Greased a pig? Worked underground?"

"I've worked an air..."

John Clark and John Roskelley at the entrance to the Pend Oreille Mine, northeast Washington, 1968. (Photo by Chris Kopczynski)

"Shut up and listen. You stay with me. I want to feel your hot breath on my butt all day. Understand?"

"Yes-s…"

"Shut up and listen. If I can get you through today, you might stay alive for a while. Don't count on keeping all those long fingers, though."

The crew sauntered out the door into the frosty air. Rupp had the vehicle, an old diesel Euclid dump truck converted to propane, waiting for us. The cab had been removed with a blow torch, the fenders beefed up with hunks of I-beam steel, and the dump bed removed. In the old steel bed's place was a flatbed of timbers with two-by-twelve side planks. We climbed aboard.

"You're going to lose that arm, son," someone said in the darkness.

I quickly pulled everything back inside the two-by-twelves.

Rupp ground the gears and drove into the tunnel.

I moved to the end of the truck bed and turned on my powerful headlamp. The tunnel was narrow. A groundhog must feel the same claustrophobia crawling into his burrow. A lot of wood and steel had been rubbed away along the side of the truck from the rock and tight corners. It was eerie. Occasionally, we entered huge caverns called "stopes," where thousands of tons of ore had been removed years before. We corkscrewed into the mine for thirty minutes before reaching the bottom.

John eased out from the truck bed and gave the day's orders to the crew, a sullen bunch with nothing to say; it was as if the depth of the mine had taken their spirit and they were already living in their private hell. I stripped to my coveralls, adjusted my headlamp, and asked myself just how I got into this mess.

Although the temperature was twenty-five degrees Fahrenheit at the surface, it was a humid eighty degrees at the bottom of the mine. Boeing 727-sized turbo fans pumped air down to us and sucked the bad air out. The tunnel floors were water-filled, leading somewhere and nowhere. All I could see was what my focused point of light showed me. For days, I would bump my miner's helmet along the tunnel walls until I adjusted my personal space to the tight walls and low ceilings of the mine.

"Grab that air drill, boy, and follow me," John ordered.

I stood the ninety-pound rock drill with air leg onto the four-foot drill bit, squatted, leaned it on my shoulder, and stood up. It was the rustiest, greasiest hunk of iron I'd ever seen.

"Where to?" I asked.

John led off in a Charlie Chaplin–like gait with a limp. Mining accidents no doubt. He found a couple of fifty-foot sections of one-inch air hose, threw them over my shoulder, and continued down a lengthy tunnel into the darkness. He was searching the side walls for something.

"Put 'er down here, boy," he said. "Go grab me a 'pig.' There's one back there."

"What's a 'pig' look like?"

"Like your girlfriend's ass! It's round and greasy and connects between these hoses, here," I was informed.

By the time I returned, John had connected all the hoses and drill together. He quickly inserted the "pig," a grease lubricator for the air hoses and drill.

"Ya know how ta work this air leg? Never mind, I'll show ya."

I had worked rock drills and air hammers before, but the air leg was a new one. Within several minutes I could have figured it out, but I wasn't about to argue. I helped John stand the drill on the leg with the bit up against the tunnel wall.

"Stand back, boy," he warned. "These things can be touchy."

I noticed early that ol' John was not the picture of coordination. He reminded me of a sloth without any joints. In fact, at his age and with his injuries, he seemed dangerous to himself. But, again, I wasn't going to say anything. Looks can be deceiving.

The valve that regulates air flow into the piston of the leg was stuck. John hit it a few times easily, then gave it a good blow with his hand. The leg blew out of the casing several four-foot lengths, shooting the drill to the tunnel ceiling. John instantly lost control. I dived for the side wall as the ninety-pound drill hit the end of its extension and fell like a giant sequoia into the tunnel. The drill hit the ground before ol' John made his first move to react. If it had fallen the other way, he would have been crushed.

I had never heard the kind of language John used that morning. It took me years to learn just some of its meaning. As luck would have it, the air leg's attachment to the drill was broken and it would have to be rewelded to the drill.

"Get me a wrench, boy," he stammered.

John removed the air leg from the drill. I thought this would end my drilling lesson and I could start another job. But I was wrong. He was going to drill that hole or die. I figured the latter was more likely.

John found a wet, moldy sawhorse up the tunnel and placed it near the wall with its long side perpendicular to the slope of the tunnel. I wasn't quite sure why he placed it in such an unstable, tipsy position, but I soon found out.

"Stand up on that 'horse,'" he ordered, "and I'll han' ya the drill."

I looked at him like he was crazy, but all he could see was my headlamp in his eyes, and that pissed him off.

"Sum-ma-bitch!" he yelled. "Keep that god-damned light to the ground! Get up there!"

This was going to be tricky. I climbed onto the top of the horse, got my balance, and reached for the drill. John was strong, but had a hard time lifting the greasy drill four feet off the ground to my waiting arms. He then somehow managed to climb onto the other end and stand up.

"Put that bit on your shoulder and jam it up against that X on the wall," he said.

The horse was unstable. Each time one of us moved, a leg would lift off the sloping floor of the tunnel and I would quickly readjust my weight to get it back. John was oblivious to the sensation.

An air drill turns the shaft of the drill bit, which in turn chips and grinds a hole in the rock. I held the shaft. I also knew that when John pulled the air valve, a whole lot of shaking was going to take place. I didn't like having that shaft in my hands, over my shoulder, and under my ear, not to mention having my face next to the working end of a diamond bit.

He pulled the valve. The horse tipped and started over as the bit kicked and bounced off the wall, throwing us off balance. I reacted instantly, got out from underneath the flailing bit with a shuck-and-dive move, and dove for the uphill side of the tunnel. I lit in a crouch, turned, and watched John.

John still hadn't figured out the horse was going down. The drill, all of it, was now in his hands, a scene reminiscent of old war films where a mortally wounded soldier stands up and continues to fire his machine gun as he keels over dead. John never bent a joint or made a move to catch himself. He, along with his horse, toppled down the tunnel still holding and firing the ninety-pound drill.

I was hoping he had broken something so that I could escape from his insanity, but no such luck. He got up off the rock, brushed himself off, and began yelling.

"What the hell did you let go of the bit for?"

"The sawhorse…"

"Shut up and listen," he growled. "We're going to get back up there again. This time, hold on."

I picked up the sawhorse, retrieved the drill, and we repeated the process. The exact same thing happened, except this time the sawhorse's leg broke. That seemed to do it. John was through. I carried the drill and air leg through the tunnel system to the truck, and John disappeared to the surface for repair work. I felt lucky to have survived my first hours in the mine.

Survive I did. In fact, I found working thirteen hundred feet underground a daily challenge. Ol' John finally, grudgingly, admitted to others on the crew I was "one hell of a worker." I carried a lot of steel and packed a lot of cement into holes for that praise, and I was proud of it.

Chris and I eventually worked together as a team underground. It was important in the mine that you knew what your partner was thinking and going to do. Unlike John, a danger to himself and others because of his age and attitude, Chris gave me a sense of security and safety. Our climbing experiences, such as on the East Face of Chimney Rock, provided us with a sixth sense for predicting each other's movements and thoughts. Neither of us was badly injured during our employment in the mine, though others on our crew were not so lucky.

As I was walking in a tunnel one morning on the way to get steel, I came upon two steelworkers crouched at the side. They had been installing a long, heavy section of angle iron when one of them had dropped his end, thinking the other would also. It cost his partner three fingers, which were still in his glove.

Every job gets old, and I was glad to get back to school in September. I needed a change from the foul air and darkness of the mine and the narrow-mindedness of some of the workers. The warmth and rolling wheat fields of the Palouse country of Washington, along with a few coeds, did a lot for my morale.

Lead and zinc prices hit rock bottom several years later, and the Pend Oreille Mine shut down production. It reopened briefly, then closed permanently in the mid-seventies. Flooding in the mine from the backwaters of Boundary Dam on the Pend Oreille River made it impossible to ever open the lower levels again.

My experience in the mine influenced my life in more than one way. When I returned to Washington State University after the job, I changed my major from business to geology. And, as with mountain climbing, there was something about working in that mine that challenged me and gave each day a purpose. The mine proved to me that there had to be more in life than a desk, a paycheck, and a steady meal.

BY LIVING ON THE SANDS OF THE RIVER AMONG
CAMPIES, WE AVOIDED THEFT, FEDERAL POLICE, AND
TALK OF HEROIC ASCENTS OF THE PAST AND TALES OF
HORROR TO COME THAT GREW LIKE JACK'S BEANSTALK
NIGHTLY AROUND CAMP IV FIRES.

A BRIEF STAY IN THE VALLEY

"How do you plead?"

"Guilty, your honor," Chris replied.

"Your privilege to use Yosemite National Park is hereby suspended for ninety days. You have eight hours to leave the park. Next case."

The verdict washed onto Chris Kopczynski like a wave of nausea. It was embarrassing to be placed in the same league as the degenerate, long-haired transients within the Yosemite National Park courtroom waiting for trial, but the verdict was fair. Chris Kopczynski and I had been caught camping within Camp VII, a

46

"trailer only" camp along the Merced River. We avoided detection for most of June by changing camps frequently and, like predators, using the early and late hours to come and go.

Yosemite Valley was filled with tourists in late June 1970, like jelly beans in a jar, and now our forest green two-man A-frame tent, pitched on the white sands of the Merced, stood out among the Winnebagos, Securities, and Cavemans like the Valley's guru, Yvon Chouinard, walking through Camp IV. While we were on our daily crack climb away from the bustle of road and trail, a benevolent Scamper Camper owner reported two suspicious "hippies" camping near his site to Yosemite park rangers. Chris and I may have looked like flower children with our collar-length hair and full beards, but our down-to-earth, Spokaneite redneck philosophy oozed out every pore. It must have showed. Real hippies shied away from us like we were DEA agents.

I approached our "campsite" on returning from crack climbing on El Capitan's Southwest Face at midmorning. The tent was gone. Out of the trees and from behind a camper appeared two rangers. Within minutes Chris and I were separated and questioned and our answers compared. Smart move on their part—our stories didn't add up. Chris, thinking I would give them a song and dance, told them we had been camped on the river only a few days. "We weren't supposed to camp here?" he asked innocently.

I told them the truth. "Camp IV sucks. If you want us to camp there, then clean it up."

They arrested him.

Living and climbing in Yosemite was as close to a life in Camelot as one could get—without Guinevere. But as the Valley filled with campies, tourists, and hippies on summer vacation, the dream ended, and I found myself in a mini-borough of Los Angeles, complete with nonstop traffic, grocery store lines, and irate urbanites. We were supposed to stay in Camp IV, a tent-only camping area, which was filled to capacity with transient climbers and drugged-out "flower children." That wasn't our scene. Theft was rampant throughout the park, but within Camp IV it was epidemic. And disease. Herpes was as common as love beads, making sex another form of Russian roulette.

At twenty years old I was more than eager to enjoy spending some time with the ladies, but smart enough to know that some of them would give me the "gift that keeps on giving"—something incurable and hideous, I was sure. I didn't chance it. Not that I wasn't tempted. To me, sexy was a blonde, long-haired California girl with a body molded and toned to thoroughbred proportions from months of living outdoors, eating brown rice and avocados and drinking herb teas. And they were everywhere. The young "old ladies" had no inhibitions. There was nothing quite like having a young hippie girl saunter up to me while I sat on the granite sands of the translucent Merced River, smile, then pull her paisley-patterned dress up over her head, exposing a trim, golden tanned body without a trace of ever having worn a bathing suit. I would have gotten an A-plus in this anatomy class. It seemed like the cutest girls

John Roskelley and Chris Kopczynski taking a break from climbing cracks in Yosemite Valley, California, 1970. (Photo by Fenton Roskelley)

in the world were in Yosemite Valley during the summer of 1970, and many were caricatures of Venus.

The girls were the only thing about Yosemite I was going to miss. The midsummer heat stagnated on the Valley floor, turning it into a barbecue pit and making climbing more of a chore than it already was. Chris and I dedicated ourselves to struggling up some classic crack each morning and evening, reserving the heat of the day for Frisbee playing and tanning on the Merced. By living on the sands of the river among campies, we avoided theft, federal police, and talk of heroic ascents of the past and tales of horror to come that grew like Jack's beanstalk nightly around Camp IV fires.

My desire before leaving Yosemite for construction labor work in Washington had been to climb my first Grade VI. My sights, accuracy notwithstanding, were set on an El Capitan route such as the Nose, but finding a compatible partner proved more difficult than an ascent. Chris, my climbing partner for five years, was just as set on not climbing El Cap or any Grade VI as I was on doing so. "I get scared enough just watching you lead one crack, let alone thirty of them."

As Chris and I stuffed down several doughnuts outside the park's visitor center toward the end of June, a short, blocky climber dressed in a soiled, multicolored rugby shirt and Chouinard climbing pants with shredded knees sat down beside us.

"Hear you're looking for a climbing partner," he said, shoring up his heavily taped wire-rimmed glasses with a single flick of a finger. "I'm up for the West Face of the Leaning Tower myself. Want to give it a try?"

It wasn't El Cap. But then again, I wasn't Royal Robbins. The West Face was considered a Grade VI only by virtue of its drunken lean toward the valley floor. It was definitely a VI on the first ascent, but with the bolt ladders in place, a climber would have to have an ultra-tight scrotum to brag "VI" in 1970. Optimistically, we planned to climb the wall in one bivouac.

Jim, a muscular block as broad as he was tall, had recently been released from the Army, and was hiding out from reality in the Valley. "Couldn't get myself killed in the Army; maybe I can get it here."

I began to wonder if I had committed myself too far this time, but I wanted the climb badly enough to take the chance.

Loaded with racks of hardware, two ropes, food, and bivouac gear, Chris, Jim, and I climbed up a talus gully to a four-foot-wide ledge that split the lower, broken cliffs of the Leaning Tower from the upper magnificent sweep of granite, which rose at a frightfully overhanging 105 degrees.

"This is as far as I go," Chris said. "Good luck."

I felt my confidence descend with Chris as he stepped back cautiously, as if to remove any possibility of contamination by stupid germs, turned, and distanced himself from Jim and me. A glance at Jim, a Barney Rubble look-alike, and I wanted to shout, "Unnncle!" and join Chris, but it was too late. If I ever wanted to show my face in the Valley again, I was committed.

I grabbed a sixty-pound haul bag, slung it over my shoulder, and squeezed behind a dead twelve-foot Sierra pine blocking an easy ledge access to the center of the face and the route's first bolt ladder.

"What-the-he... Heeeelp!" I screamed in pain. Frantically, I threw down my load, smacking and rubbing every inch of my legs, arms, and body as tiny, voracious fire ants swarmed beneath my clothing. I made moves on that narrow ledge, killing ants and removing clothing, that would have made Michael Jackson stand in awe. Naked, I plucked the little buggers from even the deepest cavities. Pinhead-sized red welts resembling bee stings rose from every bite, leaving me with what looked like a bout of chicken pox. I put this down in my mental book as another Yosemite "objective" danger, along with manzanitas, federal police, and hippie chicks. Jim may have looked like Barney Rubble, but he outsmarted me. He climbed down below the tree, leaving the ants hungry and lonesome.

Jim suggested that we lead two long bolt pitches before nightfall, rappel off, and bivouac on the ledge. That wasn't quite the way I had interpreted the guidebooks' recommendation.

"Most parties just start up early in the morning and bivouac on the upper ledge," I said.

*John Roskelley leading a difficult pitch on the Lost Arrow Spire, Yosemite Valley,
1970. (Photo by Chris Kopczynski)*

Jim grunted something about not "giving a shit" and began leading the first pitch, a seemingly endless series of expansion bolts in the crackless, tilted rock desert above me. I followed dutifully, then led the next bolt ladder to the hanging belay. The Valley took on a new dimension from where I sat hugging three itsy-bitsy anchor bolts that moved when I did. As Jim cleaned my carabiners from the bolt hangers, I mentally withdrew from my predicament, "Barney's" presence, and that of the horizontal world, and focused on the ethereal effects of space below and the sweep of granite above. For a few brief minutes I felt the exhilaration a cliff swallow must feel as it dive-bombs among the cliffs. I no longer felt trapped by gravity and doomed to spend my life walking on the surface of the earth. I was now part of a different plane.

We pushed hard the next morning, as if we were a "team," but that really wasn't the case. Jim and I were two bodies and spirits never to become one, unlike Chris and me. Jim's and my paths had crossed for no other purpose than to hold the rope for each other. I had my reasons for fighting gravity and living in the Valley—Jim had his.

Climbing demands a solid rapport with your partner, a genuine camaraderie, and a respect for the danger. Our rapport was distant, and as the climb progressed, I realized Jim had no fear, thus lacking a safety check on his other emotions. He was just plain dangerous. From that realization on, I wanted off the Leaning Tower and back with Chris.

By early afternoon, we sat idly on the first good ledge, the one most parties enjoy for their first bivouac. "Enjoy," meaning actually sleeping on terra firma. Anything above the ledge was a "hanger," a night out in your "Robbins" hammock. Jim had one. I didn't.

"Why don't we bivy here, Jim?" I asked, more as a plea than a suggestion. "We'll reach the top tomorrow no matter what."

"Go ahead," he replied, "I'll see you tomorrow night."

I wasn't equipped to solo. "Okay," I said. "I'm coming." But I didn't like it.

Each climb has its distinguishing landmarks: a move, a bivouac, even a pitch on the route that imprints itself on the mind of the climber. The Steck-Salathe on Sentinel Rock has the Narrows; the Eiger North Face has the Ice Bulge; Everest, the Khumbu Icefall. Late in the afternoon, as fading light issued dark warnings across the granite walls, I reached the Leaning Tower's landmark, Evil Tree, the dead remains of a massive, scraggly Sierra pine that had stretched its tentaclelike branches from the heart of a horizontal crack beneath an overhang toward the sun's energy—and lost. The light disappeared as I fought my way into Evil Tree's branches, anchored the rope, and waited for Jim.

"Bivouac" is an ugly word when one is unprepared. As Jim unfolded his Robbins hammock, attached it carefully to two strong tentacles, and moved in for a night's rest, I sat at the anchors, knees to the wall, shaking my head and repeating over and over to myself, "I told you so. I told you so. I told you so."

And there I hung like carrion gripped by a mighty vulture's talons, hanging from the branches, my rear planted in my belay seat, my shoulders supported by Jim's homemade one. Only my ass was comfortable, as my legs dangled with so much finality. I tried to balance my head against the haul bag, an act not unlike trying to balance a golf ball on the wrong end of a tee.

Hung for the night, I pondered the question we all come to grips with at these times: "Why?" Those of us who can't answer this question have continued to climb year after year, as if our suffering will eventually show us the light. I'm still climbing and still pondering.

I swore the next morning, as I jealously peeked at Jim snoozing comfortably, swaddled head to toe in his hammock, that I would never again set foot on a multiday climb without a hammock to comfort me at night. I lied to myself. Never again is too long and my memory too short.

Jim and I summited at midmorning, surfacing from the depths of our granite wall. Several hours later we separated in Camp IV, never to see or hear from one another again. This was to our advantage, I'm sure.

I wanted nothing more to do with cracks, climbers, or big walls. Besides, trouble within Yosemite Valley with transient flower children had brought in federal park police. These guys weren't your ordinary rangers and city cops. They were toughs. Big, mean, no-shit police, taught to harass, control, and intimidate. It was easy duty manhandling draft dodgers, hippies, and climbers (often one and the same), who all thought of the valley as a home base for getting high (in both senses). Poke a baton in a gaunt hippie's ribs; who cares? Pull 'em in and check for 'Nam dodgers. Get a little "feel" off a flower child, but watch for lice.

The feds woke with the chickens and then circulated through overcrowded Camp IV on horseback. Using bullhorns, they warned the twenty or more campers in each site, "I want to see six people in this campsite in twenty minutes or you're all going to jail."

The smell of some of those sleeping bags being opened up was enough to move the horse back a few paces. Then out from the tattered remains of a khaki-colored World War II army bag would emerge a long-haired "person," some with the hygiene of a cockroach. Once into shreds of bell-bottoms and hallucinogenic pirate shirts, the displaced would drift down the road to the Yosemite Lodge cafeteria for a fifteen-cent coffee and a plethora of refills, or to Degan's store to bum a quarter from a tourist or steal something to eat for breakfast. The feds would be back twenty minutes later, using their batons to smack the feet of those still in their bags, and hauling off to jail those who wanted to discuss "rights." That's why Chris and I chose to pitch our tent along the Merced and within the trailer camp. There were no feds, no lice, and, originally, no trouble.

We had decided to leave Yosemite the night before Chris's arrest. That night, Chris and I walked over to the big meadow. Hundreds of hippies were smoking dope, drinking cheap wine, and popping pills. Children with names like Sunrise and Moonbeam hung around their "old man" and "old lady," who were at best eighteen years old, slapping at mosquitoes and scratching skin the color and texture of fir bark. Hungry eyes, like those of yearling fawns in late winter, peeked at us from behind ankle-length skirts.

We circulated from group to group, listening to all the potential Arlo Guthries who played an instrument and sang ballads and blues to the high-pitched shrill of the crickets. One thin, hawk-nosed hippie caught our attention with his rendition of an old Peter, Paul and Mary song. Here, I thought, was a potential artist, but in Yosemite in 1970, he was just a one-dollar life with a five-hundred-dollar guitar. We entered the circle.

As Chris and I sat down, I singled her out. She was young, maybe sixteen, and pretty. Her left arm held a baby wrapped in tie-dyed cloth, suckling quietly on her breast. In her right hand was a joint. With eyes squeezed shut, she inhaled a long "toke," breathed deeply, held it, then slowly released the smoke. She passed the weed to her "old man." Did we really awake in the Age of Aquarius or just think we did?

As the ballad ended, I heard horses' hooves on pavement in the distance and the blow of excited nostrils. The guitarist chose another tune and started to play. There was something about all that noise that made me nervous. Once before I'd heard that many horses blowing, snorting, and stomping. It was in the movie *The Charge of the Light Brigade*. Just as I was about to leave the circle of hippies and investigate, the meadow exploded in excited voices, thundering hooves, and beams of light.

In a scene right out of the movie, excited and confused horses with baton-wielding riders charged upon the groups encircled about each fire. A bullhorn blared from the meadow's edge. "You are to clear the area! Clear the area! You are in violation of Yosemite Park regulations!"

The area emptied quickly. Shouting feds and angry hippies replaced the wail of harmonicas and the soft twang of guitars. Everywhere bodies were moving into the darkness to avoid the roundup. Anyone too doped or drunk to move was "captured," arrested, and dragged off to jail. Chris and I grabbed a staggering "doper," to help him out, cleared the meadow, and headed for camp. On the way I couldn't help asking Chris, "Are we still in America or what?" He didn't reply.

It was the first time, but not the last, that the rangers and feds would cavalry-charge the growing number of hippies in Yosemite. The main crackdown came a week later, on Fourth of July weekend. Hundreds were arrested, convicted, and bodily removed from the park.

Chris and I were long gone by then. We had hitchhiked into Berkeley and, with our remaining funds, purchased new ten-speed Peugeot bicycles to ride twelve hundred miles to Spokane.

"Hey, it's cheaper than a bus ticket and we have bikes in the end," Chris said enthusiastically.

He never said anything about blisters on my ass, a steady Pacific Coast gale in my face, logging trucks, weirdos, hay fever, and weeks of struggle. I almost cried thirty miles northwest of Berkeley when the pain in my butt and the extent of our idiocy became apparent. No matter how hard I pleaded, the shop wouldn't take the bike back, so north on Highway 1 we pedaled, with me whining as loud as the wind and Chris repeating every few miles, "Complaining won't do you any good."

He was right. I finally took his advice and quit whining, although by that time we were only ninety miles from home and my mother was on her way to pick us up. Better late than never.

'JOHN, YOU HAVE ABSOLUTELY THE LONGEST TOES I
HAVE EVER SEEN. A HALF INCH OFF HERE AND THERE
SHOULDN'T MAKE THE LEAST DIFFERENCE,'
RENNIE SAID OPTIMISTICALLY.

IN THE FOOTSTEPS OF HERZOG

The blast of wind cracked over the North Ridge with the authority of a bullwhip, then rushed the camp as an invisible wave. After eight days of monotonous roar from near one-hundred-mile-per-hour winds, the crack signaled something ominous, even deadly.

Caught on the slope a few yards from my tent, I spun from my chore of chopping camp ice and faced my enemy. I was too late. The gust lifted me, then hurtled me backwards into a rock wall above our camp, but not before I had seen all four poles holding up my tent snap. The expedition A-frame tent flattened as though it had been stepped on by Godzilla.

I rolled to my stomach, then spread-eagled on the snow to stop myself from disappearing down the slope with odds and ends of equipment. Tiny ice balls sandpapered my face as the wind chill bit at the ends of my ears and nose. As quickly as the gust had come, it was gone. Only the wind's steady roar over Dhaulagiri's summit ridges remained.

On the tenth day the wind died. Lou Reichardt, Nawang Samden Sherpa, two high-altitude Sherpas, and I emerged from our battered tents at Camp III, elevation 24,600 feet, and climbed upward. Our motivation was as broken as the high-strength aluminum poles that lay twisted and useless in the tent sleeves. After ten days of sedentary existence, feeling the stress of the storm and the effects of high altitude, our muscles were listless and atrophied.

Slowly, our strength and renewed vigor returned with exercise and the anticipation of completing the climb. Despite living for more than two weeks above the "Death Zone," the altitude where the human body can only deteriorate, Reichardt and I were still determined to reach the 26,795-foot summit, the sixth highest in the world.

Our team of sixteen Americans, including Reichardt and me, had spent from mid-February to mid-May of 1973 working our way west to Dhaulagiri and up its Northeast Ridge, known as the Swiss Route after the first ascent team in 1960. Seven prior expeditions to the world's sixth-highest peak had failed due to high winds, cold, and death before the Swiss success. Weather and approach difficulties were only two good reasons why Dhaulagiri, known as the "Mountain of Storms," was the first 8,000-meter peak to be reconnoitered and the last to be climbed. Thirteen years after the first ascent, only one other expedition had reached its stormy summit, the 1970 Japanese expedition. We intended to be the third.

Reichardt, a veteran of several expeditions to Alaskan peaks and one of America's most experienced high-altitude climbers, had climbed on Dhaulagiri before. In 1969, he was a member of an American team attempting the Southeast Ridge. Early in the expedition, he and seven companions—five Americans and two Sherpas—were overwhelmed by an enormous ice avalanche during a whiteout while exploring a route

Nepalese porters ferrying loads over Dampush Pass on the approach to Dhaulagiri, Nepal Himalaya, 1973.

through the broken, jumbled Southeast Glacier icefall. Sensing the futility of trying to run, Reichardt had dived for a small dishlike depression in the snow. When the ice had settled, he was unscathed. Expecting the same of his companions, he looked around. The area was scoured clean. All seven climbers had been swept into crevasses and buried under tons of ice.

Reichardt is a quiet, introspective man. I didn't really get to know him despite months on the same team. To know someone takes at least some conversation. In the ten days of living in separate tents within twenty feet of each other in Camp III, we had talked only once or twice and that to obtain food from one another. He was continually reading or absorbed in some mental chess game. I had the feeling he considered himself stuck with me because we had both been assigned to the third four-man summit team and had outlasted the other climbers. Illness, weather, and lack of determination had turned the others back.

Reichardt, a Ph.D. molecular biologist and considered a future Nobel candidate, is the caricature of a mad scientist: unruly, short-clipped hair; thick glasses that he continually adjusts, twirls, or bites on nervously; friendly eyes; and a big smile. He's unusual in that he thinks before he talks.

In terms of physical fitness, Reichardt is an enigma. He never works out with weights or runs half a mile, yet his muscles match those of a professional power lifter and his endurance is legendary. Punctual, yes. Determined, without a doubt. Graceful, only when it counts.

I followed Reichardt closely one afternoon during the trek to base camp. We jogged mile after mile heavily loaded through the pine forests and rhododendrons along the Kali Gandaki River below Dhaulagiri's southern flank. I had the impression he knew where the evening's campsite would be, and since we were so far ahead of the others, I kept him in sight. I also thought he may have been trying to outwalk me—kind of a friendly competition. He was obviously in a hurry. Late in the afternoon, Reichardt stopped abruptly along the trail in front of a large stone marker. I quietly approached and stopped behind him as he stood silently reading the names of his seven dead companions chipped in granite. He was lost in thought. I left him to be with his friends once again and returned down the trail.

The 1973 Dhaulagiri Expedition's main objective was to climb the technically difficult Southeast Ridge. The route was within our abilities, but not without ice screws. Our entire supply was used up reaching the ridge's crest. We turned our efforts to the Northeast Ridge.

In groups of four, teams carried loads to higher camps and occupied them accordingly. By Camp III, at 24,600 feet, Reichardt, Terry Bech, and I were the only "survivors." During the ten-day storm, Bech, a classical cellist, descended with a draining ear infection. Only Reichardt,

Nawang Samden, the two Sherpa porters, and I were left to try for the summit out of a team of twenty-six *sahibs* and Sherpas.

Camp IV, at 25,700 feet, was at the apex of the Southeast and Northeast ridges, a hideous point of exposure placed in desperation rather than for convenience. In 1979, the fierce Dhaulagiri wind ripped a French tent from this perch with two men inside. They were never seen again.

Hastily, Reichardt, Nawang, and I hacked a mini-platform for our tent, while our two high-altitude porters dumped their loads, wished us luck, and happily left us to our fate. It took an hour of hard labor in the thin air to chip a semiflat spot that turned out to be too short and narrow for the expedition tent. The consequences would only be realized once we settled in for the night. The three of us crammed into the two-man

Porters taking a well-earned break on the approach to Dhaulagiri, Nepal Himalaya, 1973.

tent along with down bags, coats, mats, cameras, headlamps, and additional gear and clothing.

What began as a pencil-thin line of cloud to the north swelled and billowed into another massive storm front. The wind, coyly playing dead all day, started as a breeze at dusk and by nightfall erupted into full gale. Dhaulagiri had given us one day of decent weather.

We settled in for the night, jockeying into sleeping positions. By virtue of getting into the tent last, I drew the downhill, South Face side of the tent, which hung over the edge and was supported only by tent fabric. Pressed into the unsupported tent fabric by a 150-pound snoring Sherpa rolling on top of me and knowing I had a 7,000-foot drop to the glacier below, I couldn't get to sleep.

Nawang Samden was an experienced high-altitude Sherpa in his early forties. Despite smoking two packs of filterless Nepali cigarettes a day and drinking *rakshi*, a Tibetan hard liquor made from rice, until inebriated each evening, Nawang was still a "Tiger" of the snows, an honor given to the best Sherpas for their performance on big expeditions. I would rather have had one of the younger, stronger Sherpas with us for the summit attempt, but the honor of the summit with the *sahibs* went to Nawang because of his rank among the Sherpa staff. It was customary.

I extracted myself from beneath Nawang and crawled to the vestibule at the front of the tent. Forty days before, I had frost-numbed my feet while picking up loads that had been air-dropped at base camp. Now, after weeks of living at extreme altitude and climbing to Camp IV in sub-zero temperatures, they were worse. I lit one of our Bluet Gaz stoves, and for the rest of the night I heated my socks over the flame, then put them on my feet, repeating the process endlessly in an attempt to get some sensation back in them. It was useless. All my toes and perhaps both heels were frostbitten and permanently damaged.

My thoughts turned to Maurice Herzog, leader and one of the summiters on the 1950 French Annapurna Expedition. Would I, like Herzog, also lose my toes? Would it make a difference in the quality of my life? Was the summit worth the price of flesh? Had I gone too far in the quest for something so intangible?

No. The summit was only an end to the means. I wanted Dhaulagiri if only because mountaineering is the process of finishing what one begins. The damage to my feet was already done. To leave now, before completing the climb, would only sharpen and deepen the pain to come. Whatever the sacrifice, I would make it, as long as it wasn't my life.

By early morning, I wanted out of that tent. Even the intense cold and gusts of wind were preferable to more delay. Reichardt and I switched leads along the spine of the long, low-angled ridge, cresting false summits as numerous as scales on a dragon's back. Nawang followed silently, perhaps wondering if his many Buddhist gods were awake and watching over him.

We arrived on the 26,795-foot summit in early afternoon. Wind gusts up to seventy miles per hour made it difficult to stand. Despite our layers of insulated clothing, the cold reached into our souls with its long fingers and numbed any spirit left within us. We were not using bottled oxygen, which warms the body and clears the mind. Our world of wind, hypoxia, and cold was fraught with mistakes, slow and dangerous.

I clicked one shot of Nawang leaning into the wind and holding the Nepalese flag before my 35mm Fuji froze and malfunctioned. I had no feeling in my feet. My hands switched from numbness to pain to numbness as I worked with the camera, my pack, and my harness, and completed a myriad of chores a summit seems to require. Then we departed. I felt only a sense of relief for having finished the job, even if I wouldn't be in one piece at the end.

The descent tested the essence of my patience. Reichardt, having misplaced his belt in the tent the night before, was hampered by his pants falling down around his knees, and inched his way down, slowing Nawang and me to a crawl. I was sure his stumbling and awkwardness were due to increasing hypoxia, a state of oxygen deprivation. More than once, Nawang glanced toward me through his goggles with a look that said, "Even a Sherpa shouldn't have to put up with this." I had to agree.

With each passing moment, the risk of losing not only my toes, but my feet, increased.

One tug on the rope became one too many and Reichardt threatened to unrope. It was the best scenario from a safety standpoint, but I couldn't let him do it. Teammates stick together, and I knew that, once free of the rope, I would split for camp. I talked him back onto the rope and we continued on to camp at the speed of a descending glacier.

We spent another night cramped within the tent at Camp IV. Again I moved to the vestibule and worked on my frozen feet. It was useless. My toes were chalky white and dead to the touch.

As Reichardt, Nawang, and I prepared to descend the next morning, I knew I would lose my feet if I spent all day crawling down camp to camp with Reichardt in tow.

"My feet are frozen, Lou," I said. "I'm going to head for base camp. Nawang will stay with you on your descent."

Then, after a brief handshake and good-bye, I set a quick but stumbling pace for myself down the steep gully toward Camp III and base.

My descent to base camp was a nightmare. Each camp I passed through was a ghostly skeleton of its previous self. Only a few climbers remained on the mountain. Dhaulagiri's winds had destroyed tents, the route, even the morale of those climbers below.

At Camp III, Ron Fear, who would die later that year in Bolivia in a rafting accident, handed me my first mail in a month. I quietly touched and smelled each letter my wife, Joyce, had sent, then read words of love and devotion that only a long-term separation can create. In one letter, she casually mentioned she had bought us a house. It awakened me to how long I'd been gone and how our lives might have changed.

I arrived at base camp within hours after leaving Camp IV. Lou and Nawang descended much more slowly and chose to spend another night on the upper mountain at different camps—Reichardt at Camp II and Nawang with the other Sherpas at Camp I.

For me, it was over. Once steaming hot chocolate in a plastic mug was placed in my hands and a plate of mashed potatoes with gravy was put on the table in front of me, I knew life was going to get better. As a team, we had climbed Dhaulagiri, the first Americans to do so.

Expedition leader Dr. Jim Morrissey and Dr. Drummond Rennie, official team physician, inspected the damage to my feet by pinching my toes and waiting for the blood to return. It seldom did.

"John, you have absolutely the longest toes I have ever seen. A half-inch off here and there shouldn't make the least difference," Rennie said optimistically.

I recalled what my dad had said before my departure for Dhaulagiri: "Success will bring its own reward, John." I wondered if shortened feet was what he meant.

Maurice Herzog's *Annapurna* had captured my imagination early in life. It was Herzog's account of the 1950 French Annapurna Expedition to Nepal, whose original objective had been to climb Dhaulagiri, that had planted the urge to climb in me as a young boy.

His expedition, having arrived late in the pre-monsoon season, found the approach to Dhaulagiri too time-consuming and dangerous. They turned their efforts to nearby Annapurna. Herzog, along with teammate Louis Lachenal, summited in circumstances similar to our ascent of Dhaulagiri: high winds and thirty-below temperatures. Both men were badly frostbitten and had to be carried for days on porters' backs to the roadhead. Both lost toes and fingers.

Now, as I watched and felt my feet come to life in a pan of warm water, I recalled the suffering Herzog and Lachenal had endured during their long evacuation. The long, thick needles used to inject novocaine into the nerves in their necks; suppurating, pus-filled wounds; their expedition doctor Oudot, scissors in hand, trimming flesh at each train stop through India; toes and bloody bandaging swept onto train platforms. My situation, twenty-three years later, did not look much better.

"Hey, Jim," I said, "Are you going to have to cut off my toes?"

"Jesus, John, that was in the Dark Ages!"

Well, the Dark Ages had returned. The expedition was short on Demerol, the only major painkiller, and my thawed toes felt like Thor was hitting them with his hammer. Until I reached a steady source, such as in Kathmandu, I was put on large doses of aspirin and codeine. The Demerol would be saved until I could stand the pain no longer.

The day after my arrival at base, I was strapped into a *doka*, or Nepalese basket, cut so that I could sit facing away from the porter who was carrying me. A dozen strong low-altitude Sherpas were assigned to carry me the three days to the trailhead. Each would take his turn in fifteen-minute intervals, carrying me over the rugged terrain and down to Tukche, the nearest village. When one of them tired, the others lifted me in the basket, allowing the porter to change places with another. I didn't touch the ground from morning to night except to relieve myself.

Jeff Duenwald, expedition deputy leader, volunteered to accompany me through Nepal, India, and back to Spokane for medical treatment. He was a research veterinarian and lived with his wife and three children in nearby Pullman, Washington. Having worked on animals for years, Jeff knew just how to treat a young, hard-nosed climber. He also gave the most painless injections of any of the so-called experts.

The young Sherpa "Tigers" assigned to carry me to Tukche jogged along glaciers and loose moraines effortlessly, finally reaching the green slopes of Tukche's high yak pastures. Only once did one slip and dump me into the snow. His cohorts chided him until he could take it no longer and crept away into the night. Such was the fate for failing the unwritten Sherpa code to protect his *sahib*.

We arrived in Tukche, a small Tibetan-like village, on the third day. The pain of blood entering my feet and having nowhere to go through dead tissue was driving me mad. I was laid on a bed of straw in the lower level of the guest house. On the floor above me, the Sherpas and Jeff drank *rakshi* and *chang*, a homemade barley beer, to celebrate our arrival. The more drunk and rowdy they got, the more dirt fell from the ceiling into my face. It was a steady flow toward midnight. Nobody can drink a returning Sherpa under the table.

I awoke the next morning to sounds I hadn't heard for months. Birds, insects, children playing. Nature called and without crutches or a wheelchair I had to rely on the porters. Several hungover Sherpas lifted me onto one young porter who wanted the honor of carrying the *sahib*. He carried me piggyback to a four-foot-wide, but long, cattle pen behind the guest house.

The boy stumbled going through the gate. I pitched forward over his head, augering both feet and hands into the deep manure. Pain shot through my feet. Instantly, five pairs of hands grabbed me and lifted me into the air. Concern and pity showed on their faces. Sherpas, a people whose home is in the high Himalaya, know the pain and suffering from frostbite.

The young boy who had stumbled brushed the cow dung off my bandages amidst a pummeling by the others. Once the pain subsided, I laughed at the ridiculousness of my situation and the pummeling stopped while they all laughed with me.

A small, white Tibetan pony was brought to the guest house for me to ride a day to Jomsom, the district seat and the only village with a small air strip. Buddhist prayer scarfs called *katas* were wrapped loosely around our necks by all the Sherpas to safeguard our journey. Then Jeff and I, along with John Skow, a Peace Corps volunteer who had helped our expedition, and several Sherpas, left for Jomsom in hopes a plane would happen to fly in. The only other choice of travel was to Pokhara, eight days' distance, but with the advantage of scheduled air service.

A mile into the ride, I begged Jeff to stop the horse. The pain in my feet as they dangled beneath the belly of the horse was unbearable. The aspirin and codeine that had taken care of most of the pain from base camp was no longer doing the job. I asked for Demerol, a stronger painkiller.

"There's not much," he warned. "If a flight doesn't come in within a few days to pick us up, you'll run out."

"I've got to take that chance," I said.

I'll never forget the relief that swept my body as the Demerol took effect and I was released from pain for the first time in days. Dreamily, I remounted the horse, embraced its neck, and fantasized my way to Jomsom.

A chartered Pilatus Porter was sitting in Jomsom on our arrival. Luckily for us, the Nepalese Minister of Finance and his entourage were visiting the village on government business. Without a second thought, the minister invited Jeff and me to fly back to Kathmandu with him and his wife the next morning.

Once back in Spokane, I spent two weeks in the hospital to prevent infection, then a month on crutches. All my toes were frostbitten to some degree. Whereas it was the standard treatment in 1950 to remove dead tissue and blackened flesh immediately to combat infection, I simply let time dictate whether parts of my toes were dead or the flesh would heal. I eventually lost only two joints on one toe and one joint on another. I often wonder how many toes and fingers Herzog and Lachenal would have saved if their climb had been in 1973 rather than 1950.

Years later, I met Maurice Herzog in New York. It was an accidental meeting in an unlikely place to encounter a man I considered one of my heroes. We were both dressed in black tuxedos after attending a mountain photography exhibit and were exiting a large bus that had transported us to an evening dinner with Robert Redford, Billy Joel, and Christie Brinkley, among other celebrities.

A friend of mine also attending the dinner spotted Herzog and asked me, "Do you know who that gentleman is behind us?"

I glanced around to see an elegant older gentleman of obvious wealth and impeccable taste. Despite the charm and good looks of the many well-dressed celebrities around him at the event, Herzog stood out like a king among peasants. Still, I would not have recognized him.

"It's Maurice Herzog," my friend said.

As we left the bus, I waited for Herzog and his wife and introduced myself as they stepped onto the sidewalk. He immediately recognized my name. The strain of the evening on him relaxed and his warmth let me know he was delighted I had made the effort to meet him. It is not often that a childhood hero lives up to one's expectations, but Herzog surpassed mine. He was exactly as I had imagined him to be from his book—kind, cordial, a person you would like to call a friend.

Perhaps it was a coincidence that my path to the summit of Dhaulagiri, my first Himalayan peak, paralleled Herzog's on Annapurna. What had been so exciting and inspiring for me to imagine as a youth was even more so in reality. My experiences on Dhaulagiri only strengthened my conviction that climbing was a life unto itself. Despite the months of stress, cold, risk, and injury, my reward—the development of my inner strength—convinced me to seek out further adventures in the Himalaya. Twenty years later, the reward is still worth the trouble.

I COULD SEE MARTS'S EYES WIDEN LIKE THE ORBS OF AN OWL. WE WERE EXPOSED, CAUGHT ON THE OPEN SLOPE, AND GOING TO DIE.

M*A*S*H

I was warned.

"Cool it, Dad," assistant expedition leader Bob Craig said. "You're on thin ice. Ol' Pete's about to ship you back to the States."

I knew Craig was right. Pete Schoening, leader of the first American climbing team to visit Russia, was becoming like a dormant volcano—a puff of ash here and a little rumble there. Despite Schoening's quiet, contemplative demeanor, I managed within two weeks to bring him to a boil and within moments of eruption. If I wanted to spend July 1974 at the international climbers' camp in the Russian Pamirs attempting new routes, Craig was right: "out of sight, out of mind" seemed like an appropriate rationale.

Schoening was a good mountaineer, if not one of the best America had produced—from the old school. I broke the first rule of the "old school" of mountaineering during the team's training climb of Mount Rainier prior to leaving for Russia. I soloed the mountain.

I had needed to call my wife, Joyce, in Spokane, and tell her when to meet the team on its descent from our week-long stay on Mount Rainier's summit. I ran down 8,000 feet from the summit to Paradise Lodge in sixty-five minutes, relayed my message, ate breakfast, relaxed, then ran and walked back to the top that afternoon. I had a great day. The crevasses were wide and deep like the sun lines in an old farmer's face, and the trail was wanded and as distinct as a gully wash.

The mountain's condition didn't matter. Soloing, even to the latrine, was unacceptable to Schoening. The Pamir team, hand-picked and machine-washed by Schoening and Craig for climbing ability, reputation, and attitude, was to be representative of America's finest. I was stretching the mold, and Schoening wasn't sure I was going to fit in.

Then I broke the second rule. A day before our planned descent of Mount Rainier for our flight to Russia, a Pacific storm of typhoon proportions hit the Cascade Range. Within hours we were belly-button deep in snow, and submerged in cloud as thick as a pillow.

Visibility barely reached the toes of our boots by morning. No longer was there a guide's highway to Paradise Lodge. In place of the trail and a vista of snowcapped peaks was a slanted sea of white, split by dark, toothless gaps, and an ever-present feeling of falling over. The key to a descent without a mishap was finding a route through the upper crevasse fields of the Ingraham Glacier.

On the first rope, weaving snakelike around gaping crevasses and hopping over smaller suspects, were former Rainier guides John Marts and Gary Ullin. With Molly Higgins and Al Steck on my rope, I followed the lead pair closely. If Marts or Ullin lost the route searching for wands, which happened frequently in the zero visibility, it was my self-appointed job to get the team back on route by backtracking and searching in the opposite direction. Plowing and stumbling through deep snow and gusty winds soon had us puffing and blowing like workhorses.

Higgins, second on my rope and bent on supplying unnecessary anchorage, let me know at every detour her thoughts about me and my parentage. I ignored her cussing and verbal garbage and focused on a safe descent. But, as ornery as I am, I may have tugged a little harder the farther we descended and the more verbal her abuse.

Once safely at Cadaver Gap, below the whiteout, and free of the storm raging on the upper slopes, I removed the rope from my harness, coiled my seventy-five-foot section to Higgins's waist, handed it to a surprised Steck, and said, "Here, you take her. I'm tired of being called a son of a bitch." Then I walked off to Camp Muir, several hundred yards away.

This time Schoening hit the roof. But still, given his personality, that's like a koala bear getting mad. Nothing happened, and he buried it inside.

Schoening finally reached the end of his long rope after my run-in with a Moscow cop in Red Square when the team first arrived in Russia. Surely he didn't expect me to take shit from a Russian cop and walk away without a protest. Did he?

He did. We were invited as guests of the Soviet state to participate with eighteen other nations in a month-long climbing camp. Our actions would dictate whether other exchanges in the future would take place. Schoening was determined to leave a good impression.

The Red Square affair happened the morning after our arrival in Moscow. The American Pamirs team, led by our assigned guide, Soviet Master of Sport in mountaineering Eugene Gippenreiter, left the hotel by bus for Red Square to change money at the State Bank.

Eugene spoke better English than I did. "Please, stay together and follow me to the Foreign Money Exchange," he ordered.

The city was teeming for so early in the morning. Russians crowded the sidewalks on their way to work or to stand in breadlines. Tourists mingled, clutched their cameras, and drifted aimlessly across the cobblestones of Red Square.

Marts and I sauntered behind our group, which weaved in and out of the crowd, obediently following the indefatigable Eugene. Like a shepherd watching his flock, Eugene constantly took a head count, so as not to lose one of his "sheep."

The early morning light on the gold domes of St. Basil's Cathedral was too tempting a photo to pass up.

"John, go ahead with the others," I said. "I'll be right there."

As Marts disappeared in the crowd, I left the sidewalk and crossed the street toward a plywood barrier protecting a street repair project. Plywood didn't quite fit the image of the cathedral I wanted to capture.

As I framed the domes through my lens, a deep, short bark of authority from beneath a massive stone wall of the cathedral caught my attention. Walking casually toward me, hands folded behind his back as if it was useless for me to run, was a jackbooted, khaki-uniformed guard, radiating a sense of arrogance that seems to come with all uniforms.

He barked another order at me as he reached my side.

"What can I do for you, pal?" I replied. I knew he didn't speak a word of English. But I didn't speak any Russian either.

"*Passporta,*" he demanded, holding out his hand.

I knew what that was. I wasn't about to hand him my passport, so with pidgin English and pantomime explained that I was only taking a photo. So was everybody else.

His dark eyes narrowed under the stiff, black-brimmed police cap. His other hand came out from behind his back with a foot and a half of serious-looking billy club that was dark brown, chipped and scratched from irritating countless railings and doors, and well-worn like his boots. He wasn't kidding.

I argued briefly before his bat, poked gently into my sternum, convinced me to hand over my passport. Then he demanded a ruble. That I didn't have. I wasn't about to be blackmailed for my own passport, so I began to argue as he walked away from me and into the street.

The Russians enjoy a show like anyone else. As I yelled and argued with the policeman, a crowd surrounded us. His bat was in my chest and my finger was in his when a middle-aged Russian man walked up to my tormentor, spoke a few words, and pointed toward a building. We all turned. There was Marts, camera in hand, hiding behind the corner of the building and photographing the conflict.

The policeman motioned for Marts to approach front and center.

"Camera," he demanded.

John balked for a fraction of a second, thought better of it, then handed it over as if he were handing a loaded gun to a child.

The officer inspected it intensely, but couldn't find the opening to get the film.

"Open," he said.

"Tell him to eat shit, John," I suggested.

Marts looked at me like I'd just asked him to shoot his brother, opened the camera and handed it back to the officer.

He pulled the film from the camera, stripped the celluloid from the protective case, parted his lips in an awry smile, and gave it back to Marts in a rat's nest. The crowd laughed and waited for the next episode.

Marts was given leave and he quickly left the scene to find Eugene. I renewed my own efforts to retrieve my passport. With the help of an English-speaking tour guide, who was leading a group of tourists through the square, I finally found out why the policeman had confiscated my passport.

"He says you crossed the street illegally," the tour guide explained. "In your country I think you call it jaywalking."

The crowd burst into laughter.

"Tell him to keep my passport," I said, and began to walk off.

"Just a minute. He wants you."

The policeman reached into his pocket for my passport, said something loudly to the crowd as he held it in the air, then handed it to me. The crowd broke out into laughter.

The tour guide translated again. "He says you can have your passport back, but next time, obey the law."

Several days later, we left Moscow. Schoening didn't mention the incident, but through Craig, I knew he was upset. Word was relayed to me as I was sitting in the center of the Russian Ilyushin prop jet headed south for Osh, Kirghizistan, that Schoening wanted to see me. He and Craig had made the final selections of climbing teams and their mountaineering objectives for our month-long stay in the Russian Pamirs. It was the moment I had been waiting for.

Nineteen of us had been chosen out of the hundreds who had applied for the opportunity to climb in the Pamirs. Schoening and Bob Craig had gotten to know each of our personalities and abilities thoroughly in the few weeks we were together, and in my case, too well.

"John," Pete began, "I'm putting you on a team to be led by Bob Craig. Your objective will be the reconnaissance of the North Face of Peak of the XIXth Party Congress."

"Right, Pete," I thought. "Check your list again."

Didn't he mean the unclimbed East Face of Peak Lenin? That was the ultimate objective in the Pamirs, not Peak Something-or-other. I was considered one of the best technical climbers in the group—a necessity on Mount Lenin judging by the photos. I was supposed to be a shoo-in.

So this was my slap on the wrist. I was to be passed over for the prime target because of my shenanigans.

Okay, I had shown a bit of exuberance here and there. But I was like a Dr. Jekyll compared to the British team of Doug Scott, Tut Braithwaite, Clive Rowland, Paul Nunn, Guy Lee, and Speedy Smith. The Russian authorities undoubtedly considered beefing up the Berlin Wall after their departure.

My stunts just happened; the Brits planned theirs. For instance, they stumbled onto an ingenious method of raising funds for their trip right in Moscow. Several purchased cartons of American and European cigarettes in the foreigners-only store, walked outside and around the corner, and sold them to passing Muscovites for twice the price. Cigarettes were like Levi's—the Russians would do anything for them.

Who knows where the KGB were when the Brits were developing free trade, but they were already on to the next stunt.

On the seven-hour flight south from Moscow to Osh, the group of international climbers was served several meals. Upon landing in Osh, we stood up to depart, but the doors to the plane remained shut. We were asked to retake our seats.

Out on the asphalt runway, one hundred twelve-year-old girls dressed in uniforms similar to American Bluebirds were lined up, waiting patiently and holding bouquets of flowers, one for each of us. It was over a hundred degrees Fahrenheit. The flowers and the girls were wilting.

After ten minutes one of the Russian translators on the plane announced over the intercom that a spoon had been stolen during lunch. No one would be allowed to leave the plane until it was returned. The air conditioning was turned off, leaving more than ninety Americans, Brits, Scots, and Japanese squirming in private pools of sweat wondering who did it.

But we all really knew. It had to be one of the Brits. The Japanese just don't do that kind of thing, and the Scots and Americans had figured on waiting until base camp to "borrow" a spoon. Someone wanted one with "AEROFLOT" stamped on it badly enough to prepare early.

Sure enough, within a few minutes, the missing spoon rattled into the aisle next to the Brits. It was snatched off the floor by an Aeroflot flight attendant, who during lunch had proven to have the same temperament as a grizzly. The doors opened.

"Who else is on the team, Pete?" I asked.

"John Marts and Gary Ullin," he replied. "Meet with Bob on the details."

I was not to be singled out. All the rebels were relegated to Peak Something-or-other. Marts and I were as thick as Pepto-Bismol and our personalities meshed like a well-tuned engine. God forgot to break the mold when the first one of us was created. We were about the same height, five feet ten inches, and weight, 150 pounds. Marts's hair was lighter blond, but our blue eyes betrayed the same intensity and humor. We could instantaneously sense fun with a potential "victim" and play with him like cats with a frantic mouse.

Just Marts's association with me had won him a place on the team. But to chisel his selection in granite he had gotten bombed on vodka in the Moscow airport prior to our departure for Osh, and Eugene, our

M∗A∗S∗H. Left to right: *Gary Ullin, Bob Craig, John Roskelley, John Marts. Russian Pamirs, 1974. (Photo by Gary Ullin)*

Mountaineering Federation contact, had shown more than a little disgust at the episode. Not to mention the fact that Schoening was a teetotaler.

Marts's selection for the Peak XIX team would be a loss to American strength on Lenin's East Face. Not only was Marts one of America's true alpinists, having completed numerous ascents on difficult routes in the Alps, such as the Walker Spur on the Grand Jorasses, but he was also a former climbing guide and a qualified emergency medical technician. I was glad he was with us.

Gary Ullin had shown a bit too much "spunk-nik" also. Marts and I admitted Ullin into our group and shared our esprit de corps, despite the fact that he was the only one of the three of us who had a steady job. He was a United Airlines navigator, edging up yearly in rank to that of pilot.

Ullin knew he had directed his world where he wanted it. Educated, employed, talented, and athletic, he wore his confidence as easily as his well-pressed and fitted airlines uniform. If you were to line up our team of nineteen Americans and guess what each did for a living, Ullin would still come out with a seat in a cockpit. I could picture Ullin strutting into a Boeing 737, hat tipped forward to hide his premature balding, mustache waxed, joking with the flight attendants as they prepared for the passengers. Ullin was a bit more careful than we were as to his pranks, but obviously shunned authority. Along with his strength and experience, we wanted him for his ribald stewardess jokes. When stuck in a tent during a storm, that kind of humor turns golden.

Ullin was no slouch in the climbing world either. He didn't have the international reputation Marts and I did, but he had completed routes throughout the United States, South America, and Alaska that definitely qualified him for Mount Lenin. His addition to our Peak XIX team made our group one of the strongest in the Pamirs that summer.

Bob Craig is a prime candidate for a segment on *60 Minutes*. Reminiscent of Ichabod Crane, Craig stands as tall as an oak tree and would stretch even higher, but like a giant oak he bends deeply at the shoulders, cutting his height by several inches as if to apologize for it. His features are large and rugged, beginning with his plate-sized hands with rootlike fingers, feet that no boot will fit, a thick chest, long storklike legs, and a Jimmy Durante nose. These rough features tend to make most men shy and introverted, but not Craig. He uses them to make one at ease in his presence, along with puppy-kind eyes and an easy smile to let you know he's sincere.

At first, I thought Craig was along to raise money for expedition expenses and smooth the way as we entered Russian territory. It seemed like every time he got near a phone he was on it like a bookie working

Churchill Downs. I half expected to see him pull out a phone during the climb and check up on whatever it was he was always checking up on. But later I realized Craig was much more valuable as a people person, someone with advice—and there was no question we needed some.

Craig was smooth. Women liked him, probably because he was like a father figure. The Russians liked him because he was unassuming and nonintimidating. In fact, I liked him. He was a good climber, having climbed extensively in the continental United States, Canada, and Alaska. Craig was a member of the 1953 K2 Expedition and known as a cool customer under pressure. When he wasn't on the phone or buddying up to our Russian friends, Craig could be all laughs.

"Big Daddy," as Craig was affectionately called by our team, considered himself an alter ego to Pete's leadership. At fifty years old, he was surprised to be put in control of any team, let alone the three of us. He had his hands full, somewhat like Ben Hur and his team of three charging chariot steeds. Craig needed to loosen our reins, let us run, ease into the corners, and pray he was still aboard at the finish.

We called ourselves "M*A*S*H," after the popular, long-running television series. Like the program's characters, we were good, but didn't take rules and regulations too seriously. It was why we were together and why we were given Peak XIX. It was just a stepping-stone to the East Face of Peak Lenin as far as we were concerned. Once we finished off our "assigned" objective, we would knock off the big one. Pete couldn't object to that.

The Russians went out of their way to make life comfortable for the 180 climbers from nineteen nations attending the climbing camp in the Pamirs. Each national contingent was given the use of Polish two-man pup tents at base camp, set up in long rows surrounding the ceremonial area. Peak Lenin (23,406 feet) and Peak XIX (19,423 feet) provided a stunning backdrop above the "Glade of the Edelweiss" and base camp. Trees were nonexistent, but the grasses were so green and thick and the edelweiss so white and tall that many of the Kirghizia ponies seemed to have contented grins on their faces.

We ate in shifts while at base camp. By far the largest contingent of climbers was the sixty Austrians. They ate on the first shift by right of sheer numbers and having arrived in camp a day earlier than we had. I made the mistake of getting in line for lunch with them the day of our arrival and was soon made aware of the theory of the territorial imperative. I felt like an impala at a lions' convention.

The rest of us ate on the second shift. Besides the ample amounts of fish, black bread, kasha, fresh fruits, and borscht, red sturgeon caviar was standard at every meal and, as far as I could tell, tasted like lumpy body oil beads. In addition, vodka and Georgian wines were available at the commissary for a few rubles. And, as usual, any time climbers and alcohol get together for more than a casual toast, more mountains and big routes get climbed inside a tent than out. The Pamirs camp was no exception.

The top Russian men climbers were in camp as "advisors." They occupied tents near the mess and movie theater tents. Across the creek from the 180 foreign "devils" was the Russian women's climbing team. They were all business. Each morning at base camp we crawled from our canvas tents to the sight and sound of the women's team doing calisthenics, all dressed alike in blue warm-up suits.

Discipline. They lived on it. It permeated the air anytime I was near them. It's why for many decades other nationalities have captured a few medals at the Olympics and the (former) Eastern bloc countries have stumbled back home under kilograms of gold. Americans have asked themselves every four years how we could lose to the (former) Soviet Union. We have such high regard for our abilities and training and then can't believe it when we get beat at our own games. Discipline and teamwork—the Russians excel at them.

The Russian women were in camp for one purpose—to make the first all-women ascent of Peak Lenin by a new traverse up the Lipkin Route and down the Razdelnaya Route. They would be in competition with four women who had formed their own international team—two from Switzerland and one each from Germany and the U.S. The prize was eventually not worth the sacrifice. Nine of the twelve women in the two groups died on Peak Lenin that month.

▲ *John Roskelley practicing aid techniques in the Washington Cascades, 1967. (Photo by Chris Kopczynski)*

◀ *John Roskelley, with the West Face of Ojibway, Montana's Cabinet Range, in the background, 1966. (Photo by Chris Kopczynski)*

▼ *John Roskelley preparing to descend from Gladsheim Peak in the Valhalla Range of British Columbia, 1966. (Photo by Chris Kopszynski)*

*John Roskelley leading on the ▲
West Face of the Leaning
Tower, Yosemite Valley, 1970.
(Photo by Chris Kopczynski)*

*Bob Christianson focusing on ▶
the next objective, on the
summit of Mount Assiniboine,
Canadian Rockies, 1968.*

Lou Reichardt, one of America's strongest high-altitude climbers.

▲ Dhaulagiri (26,795 feet), the world's sixth highest peak. The expedition's route is the center ridge, rising right to left. (Photo by Jeff Duenwald)

▼ The 1973 American Dhaulagiri Expedition in Pokhara, Nepal.

▲ *The international climbing camp in the Russian Pamirs, with the North Face of Peak XIX rising from the valley, 1974.*

▼ *John Marts and Bob Craig, Peak XIX.*

▲ *Gary Ullin on Peak XIV.*

◄ *Bob Craig, climber, assistant leader, all-American promoter, addressing a gathering of international climbers, 1974.*

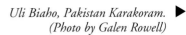
Uli Biaho, Pakistan Karakoram. ▶
(Photo by Galen Rowell)

◀ *Jim States doing what he loves best—climbing in impossible conditions, 1980.*

▼ *The frozen waterfall, Bourgeau Left Hand, Banff National Park, Alberta, Canada.*

◀ *Kim Schmitz in his hammock soaking up morning sunshine on Uli Biaho, 1979.*

◀ *Balti porters in Skardu, Pakistan.*

▼ *Kim Schmitz on Uli Biaho, 1979.*

Only one of the Russian women, Elvira Shataeyeva, spoke English. She was a medium-boned, vivacious blonde with blueberry eyes, a mountain tan, and an arousing accent. She was one of those people who feels at ease around others and draws you to her.

Elvira organized and led all-women teams in the mountains, not as a challenge to men, but as the next step in their development as athletes, following naturally upon their previous accomplishments. Her climbing accomplishments indicated her purpose. In 1973, she led the first all-women ascent of a 7,000-meter peak, Peak Eugenia Korzhenevskaya (7,105 meters). The next year, she led another women's expedition on a traverse of the Ushba. Peak Lenin was another step for her and her teammates as a test for themselves.

Elvira was seldom alone when she graced the mess tent in the evening. Climbers from every nation enjoyed her easy conversation and uninhibited laughter. But late one evening I found her sitting alone in the corner of the tent and, uncharacteristically for me, I sat down across the table from her to talk. It was as if I'd known her all my life.

"I have been curious about you," she said as I was about to leave for bed. "Where are you from in your country?"

"The state of Washington on our west coast," I replied.

"Aaah," she said, as if everything now made sense. "I thought you were from the west. I have always wanted to meet an American cowboy and I knew you must be one."

Her image of a cowboy was from old American movies starring John Wayne, Gene Autry, and others. Dressed in jeans and sporting long, thick sideburns, I looked the part and fit her perception of the west. I left it to her imagination and said good night. I never saw her again.

Elvira and her teammate, Galina Perehodyuk, were the last of the eight Russian women on Peak Lenin to perish of hypothermia during a ferocious storm. I was poised below Peak Lenin that evening at a rescue camp when the radio crackled for the last time. Through the static and wind I could hear Galina's voice weakly reaching out to all of us. Elvira must now have been too weak to talk.

It was August 8, 8:30 P.M. The hand-held walkie-talkie hissed like a cobra. The storm, thousands of feet above us, raged over the high-pitched voice on the radio. Hysterically on the edge, but still in control, Galina fought for composure.

As if speaking within a tunnel, Galina said in Russian, "Now we are two. And now we will all die. We are very sorry. We tried but we could not.... Please forgive us. We love you. Good-bye."

I could picture Elvira in my mind then and I can still imagine her now, struggling to sit out in the open of the storm despite the one-hundred-miles-per-hour winds that whipped across the semi-flat plateau below Peak Lenin's summit. Storm-induced blackness enveloped the two women as Elvira hugged her soon-to-be-dead comrade, as if needing to die touching another human being. She clutched the small plastic radio with the palms of both hands, hands that could no longer function. There was need to panic, yet resignation that it would do no good. Blood no longer moved freely through her hands and feet. She was quickly reaching the point where death was a relief, not a fear.

I can hear Galina's voice to this day. Elvira's and her resignation to death toward the end of the storm is the most haunting memory I have in twenty-seven years of mountaineering.

But before the women's tragedy, the 180 foreign climbers below the magnificent Pamirs were in a holiday mood and full of optimism. Competition between nationalities was brewing. Several strong climbing teams besides the Americans were interested in the East Face of Lenin.

The flag-raising ceremony to open the camp set British-Russian detente back another decade. Each nation had a tall, white flagpole to raise their nation's flag during the opening ceremony, and behind each flagpole stood the climbers in neat rows. A key representative from each country walked forward on request by a Russian official and raised that country's flag.

Next to us were the five Brits and four Scots, in no particular order or line. Two of them stepped forward upon request, attached a peculiar-looking "flag" on the rope, and hoisted skyward a pair of women's underwear, then stood back and saluted. The camp broke into laughter, but the Russians moved forward without a stumble. A British Union Jack replaced the underwear during the night.

After several days of ceremonies, speeches, acclimatization, and preparation, the climbing teams were ready. Most were after one route or another on Peak Lenin. Only a few groups, namely the Brits and Americans, were after alternate peaks or new routes.

"M∗A∗S∗H" was on the move after only a few days at base camp. We began ferrying loads on July 16 and 17 to the base of Peak XIX, then moved to Camp II below the massive base sliced and gouged by avalanche gullies. Every prospective route seemed swept continually by ice avalanches, the result of huge seracs separating from the upper walls.

The direct North Face would have to be the "indirect" for us. We would start to the left to avoid the gullies, then move into the center of the face as the avalanche danger minimized. The clear skies and high pressure that had characterized June were over. Unusually bad weather for July had set in, and with it, daily rain at the lower elevations and heavy snowfall on the mountain.

To climb the face, we were going to have to eliminate some of the weight from our packs. The first thing to go was "Boris," our culinary mascot. Boris, a ten-pound dried fish with guts, head, eyes, and all, contributed a few ounces of tasty meat, pounds of bone and parts, and lots of laughs to our menu, but now, extra weight was too critical.

The Russians had provided much of the climbers' food, including "Boris," and weight wasn't one of the Russians' criteria for provision. The classic dense loaves of black bread were the next to go. Black bread may have won the Eastern front for the Russians against the Nazis during World War II, but if we carried it any farther, we would never leave Camp II. Once we were down to fighting weight, we felt we had a chance to climb quickly through the high-risk zones.

We picked a safe line along the left side of the face, choosing to frontpoint technically steep and difficult ice, rather than take an easier, more avalanche-prone route. A long traverse through mushy snow took us to the center of the face. The morning was a good one. We could be on top in three days if the weather cooperated and Marts's stomach ailment, which had come on in base camp, cleared.

We perched Camp III on a shelf between two yawning canyons. There was no protection from the avalanche danger on the slopes above, and the deep, porridgelike snow made me nervous. It was thigh deep from the daily snowfall, yet thick and heavy from melting in the ovenlike heat. The air temperature, freshly fallen snow, and a gut feeling increased an uneasiness within me that even the casual cheerfulness of the team couldn't dispel.

I was motivated to set off early the next morning. We were still overloaded, and the oppressive heat in the concavity of the huge face slowed us to a crawl. To avoid crevasses, we traversed as much as we ascended, finally breaking out from the icefall onto the smooth upper face.

It was still early morning when we chose the only spot that looked reasonably safe for Camp IV. From there the face steepened and led directly to the summit. The slope at camp was twenty-five degrees, easily excavated for our two A-frame tents and semi-protected from the upper slope by an ice wall one hundred feet above. BB-like snow peppered camp until the cooling temperatures of late afternoon changed the falling snow to maple leaf–like flakes. Thunderheads swallowed the Pamirs, as they did every afternoon.

Ullin was like a young puppy among old dogs. He had too much energy. We all pitched in to set the basic camp, but Ullin couldn't sit still.

"I'm going to build a snow cave," he announced. "Anyone want to join in?"

I didn't. The slothlike beast of lethargy had wrestled me down onto my sleeping bag and won. My boots were off and I wasn't going to move. Personally, I had never built a snow cave and the only one I had slept in was cold, cramped, and dark. I was a tent man all the way.

The virtues of snow caves are known in detail. Each of us had horror stories or lifesaving accounts of holes in the snow. Ullin and Marts were "cavers," probably because the Cascades, where they did most of their mountaineering, had plentiful amounts of wet, sloppy snow great for caves. Craig and I didn't care one way or the other, except it was work and neither of us was interested.

Marts succumbed to Ullin's show of energy and helped him dig after Ullin promised to let him sleep in the cave if they got it big enough. Asses and elbows were all that could be seen of Ullin and Marts for the rest of the afternoon.

The next day we sat. The storm was a quiet one, but something eerie was in the air. Visibility was down to ten feet. We were prepared to wait out the weather if necessary, and a rest day would benefit us all. Craig kept us amused with stories of old girlfriends, while Ullin honed in on cockpit humor.

The laughter ended abruptly at noon. An immense wall of ice gave way thousands of feet above and swept the face. Each in our own way, we prepared to die. Then, just as quickly, our lives were spared. Only the ice cloud hit the camp as hundreds of thousands of tons of ice followed a gully to one side and cascaded to the base of Peak XIX, obliterating our ascent route.

It could be argued successfully that we had lost control of our own destiny. Mother Nature was obviously in full command. Casual conversation about the summit and our eventual return to base camp began with the word "if," rather than the pre-storm "when."

Just as our hearts returned to the beat of a one-half-horse engine, the earth vibrated. One moment we were eating and playing chess, and the next we were bouncing up and down in the tent. Small avalanches broke loose on all sides, but no camp-eaters.

It wasn't until a few minutes after the movement that someone acknowledged what we all knew but refused to accept. We had just sat through an earthquake rated "bladder-buster" on the Roskelley scale and were still attached to the mountain.

"There are going to be some aftershocks," I warned, remembering my geomorphology training in college.

"I hope the others climbing toward Krylenko Pass and Peak Lenin are okay," Craig said. "That was a big quake and could have set off a lot of those slopes."

We later found out that a large avalanche had hit the American group and swept some of them down with it. They all survived, although Allen Steck had sustained injuries that kept him from climbing the rest of the trip. They were lucky.

Snow continued to fall as we settled into our sleeping bags that night. Ullin finished his snow cave, but oddly enough, instead of sleeping in it as he had intended, he stashed the extra equipment inside. He and Craig slept in the expedition two-man, while Marts and I crammed into the smaller tent several feet away on the same excavated platform.

I dozed. A few minutes of sleep, then a few more. The storm outside was intense. Drifting snow locked the tent walls in place and the rhyth-

Gary Ullin and Bob Craig relaxing in the camp that was buried by an avalanche later that night, Peak XIX, Russian Pamirs, 1974.

mic flapping of nylon soon ceased. Ullin and Craig had stopped talking hours before.

Suddenly the tent ceiling collapsed.

"John, we've been hit by an avalanche," Marts said sharply through the dark.

"The tent just collapsed from snow weight," I replied.

"Well, I'm holding it up and I won't be able to hold it much longer."

"Okay, okay, I'll take a look outside if I can get the door open," I said. "I'm only partially buried."

I was sure that I was right. We had been too lazy to get out and dig during the heavy snowfall that night and deserved the inconvenience.

I heaved against the weight of the snow near the door to get some space. Prior to going to bed, I had stashed my flashlight, boots, mitts, and other clothing under and next to my head. Severe frostbite and the loss of several toes the year before on Dhaulagiri had taught me to be prepared for anything. I grabbed the cheap plastic mini-light, found the door zipper, and jerked until I had enough room to poke the light through the tiny opening.

There was nothing. No tent. No platform. No Gary or Bob. Nothing but snow slope, gusting winds, and swirling snow.

"John, can you get free?" I asked.

"No. Can you see the other tent?"

"No. It's gone."

The space that was left in the tent was Houdini's worst nightmare. I put on my boots, hat, and gloves, and squeezed from the questionable protection of the partially collapsed tent.

"Bob! Gary! Can you hear me!" I yelled. I had little hope that they were alive. They must have been carried away and into the serac jungle below.

"Here!" came a muffled response from a few feet away. It was Craig, and he had not been swept away, but instead was pinned under the heavy snow from the avalanche.

"Hang on. We're coming for you!" I yelled.

I loosened up the snow around Marts to free him, then plunged through hardpan snow over to where I could hear Craig's voice. I dug furiously to get to his face. The snow had settled like concrete. Even with mitts I was having a tough time digging.

Craig began talking. "I thought you guys had been swept away and I would die here."

"Save your air," I said.

Marts was at my shoulder within minutes. We were down to tent fabric. I could feel Craig's nose and mouth through the nylon as he turned his face.

"I haven't heard Ullin for some time," Craig yelled. "Can you get to him?"

"We'll have you free in a second, Bob," I replied. "I'm going to cut the tent."

"Don't cut the tent," Marts said. "We may need it later."

The entire scenario flashed through my mind in a millisecond—2:00 A.M., gusting winds, heavy snowfall, unclimbed face, exposure, hypothermia, two men trapped and dying. Two men ....

"To hell with the tent," I yelled.

I grabbed the fabric over Bob's face, made some space, and slit the ripstop nylon. Bob sucked in fresh air like a newborn from the womb.

"Get Ullin," he ordered.

We left Craig buried and trapped except for his face and turned to where we thought Ullin's face might be. Marts started to dig without gloves, froze his hands, then tried using his coat. I dug like a badger.

Ullin was deep. He was on the inside of the platform next to the four-foot snow wall. We hit tent fabric. Underneath was the contour of his shins. We had guessed wrong.

Marts and I moved over five feet and repeated our digging efforts, yelling for Gary to "hang on." There was no answer.

This time there was no discussion whether or not to cut the tent. I slit it like I was gutting a fish's belly. Marts continued to widen our snow hole.

Gary was unconscious and limp. I grabbed him under the armpits and heaved, pulling him out from his tomb and onto a snow mound. Marts started mouth-to-mouth, while I began CPR. We weren't going to let him die on us.

Our senses are tuned to assimilate information and allow the brain to formulate a response. The sound of a bubbling brook, the feel of a hot plate, the sight of blaze orange in the woods stimulate a reaction. This time it was our sense of smell. Marts's air blown into Ullin's lungs came back foul and inhuman, the type of dead air I would expect at the opening of a pharaoh's tomb.

Marts leaned back and glanced at me in the eerie luminescent light of falling, swirling snow. The stale odor of death was unmistakable. Gary was dead.

Our shock was short-lived. A faraway rumbling and grating sound from above alerted another sense. The sounds were growing quickly and becoming more intense. Avalanche!

I could see Marts's eyes widen like the orbs of an owl. We were exposed, caught on the open slope, and going to die.

"Jump for the hole," I yelled.

We scrambled to find a niche in Gary's former tomb. Then it hit. Marts must have felt the same fear as I because neither of us squatted completely below the protection of the wall, but stood with our upper shoulders to the force of the current, hoping to stay above the snow once it stopped and settled. If we were buried, there was no telling if we could get out.

The noise had exaggerated the size of the avalanche. It was more of a large slough, and its power dissipated on the low-angled slope. Marts and I fought and won the battle against being swept to our deaths in the seracs below. I freed my torso from the packed snow and began digging for Craig's face. Marts, who was buried deeper, soon fought his way free and joined me.

The snow had packed in around Craig's exposed face. He had once again managed to get an arm over his head to protect a small breathing area. Within minutes, we freed Craig and he crawled from the collapsed and buried tent in his thermal underwear and socks.

It's at times like this when people show their human side. It was snowing, blowing, and 2:30 A.M. Avalanches were going off all around us. We needed to find safety. Time was critical, yet we took a few precious seconds to hug each other and mourn for Gary. Luckily for us, we were still alive.

"Follow me," I said, then turned in the dark and began kicking steps toward a steep-walled serac one hundred feet above us. I felt this would provide us with our only chance of survival.

Despite the intensity of the situation, Craig didn't panic. He grabbed his sleeping bag, knickers, down parka, and the Russian radio with extra batteries. The second avalanche had buried Marts's and my tent, and with it our personal gear, mats, coats, and sleeping bags. Craig, having noticed Marts was in down booties, grabbed his and Ullin's boots before leaving the devastated campsite and following Marts and me into the darkness and storm.

After what seemed like only minutes, I reached a spot below the serac and kicked and dug a reasonable snow cave at its base. Marts, despite lacking gloves and still being in his booties, helped widen and deepen the small hole. The cave saved our lives.

Throughout the night avalanches swept over and around us. The storm raged until midday, then slowly the script changed. Storm props were no longer needed. The snow and wind stopped. Billowing clouds opened enough to allow the sun a few moments to bathe the peak.

For the first time in days, the Russian walkie-talkie worked. Craig contacted base camp early in the morning. By noon, an international rescue team was steaming its way toward Peak XIX and two Russian helicopters were en route from Osh.

We spent two nights in the cave. After excavating our own gear and retrieving helicopter-dropped equipment, Craig, Marts, and I waded through extreme avalanche slopes before exiting the face onto the Northeast Ridge on July 26. Craig, suffering back pain, and Marts, who was snowblind and had frostbitten hands, would not participate in a climb in the Pamirs for the rest of the trip. Of the four of us, I was the only one to escape unharmed.

We were met by an advance rescue team of Americans and French, who were part of a larger contingent comprising Russian, Swiss, West German, and Dutch climbers just hours behind. Our climb on what I originally thought of as Peak "Something-or-other" was over.

Postscript

I returned to finish the North Face route on Peak XIX a week later with Jeff Lowe. We entered the route from the Northeast Ridge, where Craig, Marts, and I had exited off the face. After enlarging the cave and reburying Ullin, we spent a comfortable night before completing our route on the North Face, which we named the "Ullin" route, on Peak of the XIXth Party Congress the next day.

Ullin was in the cave the night before we summited. He woke me. At first I thought it was Lowe. But Lowe was asleep. I could hear him breathing.

No, the presence I felt was Ullin. Ullin had not yet left the face of Peak XIX. His soul was still trapped amid the wreckage of Camp IV. Without knowing why, I realized our success on the face would set him free. I'm convinced it did.

A MANGLED AND RUSTY PITON, A SURVIVOR EVEN IF ITS OWNER WASN'T, INDICATED TO US THAT OTHERS HAD GONE THIS WAY—SUCCESSFULLY OR NOT.

SLIP, SLIDE, AND AWAY

The North Face of the Eiger's defensive armor, 6,000 feet of vertical, wet limestone and rock-pitted black ice, fell away beneath us. Chris Kopczynski cautiously edged backward six feet along the narrow summit cornice, focused his Rolli 35 on my tired visage, and captured evident relief as I balanced on the pointed summit.

"Take two," I said. "I don't want to have to come back for a second look."

For two and a half days we had dodged rock missiles, swum through vertical waterfalls, and shivered into the night to climb the world's most notorious rock and ice wall. Survival was our just reward.

Our arrival in Zurich on August 15, 1974, with only five days left on our thirty-day excursion tickets after the Russian Pamirs trip, eliminated the luxury of planning. Planning isn't Chris's or my strong suit anyway. The train ride through Switzerland to Grindlewald ate one day, our flight home would eat another. That left three days to climb the infamous Nordwand, a nightmare the two of us had harbored since we were sixteen. Three days! Some of the best climbers in the world take years to catch the Eiger's weather eye sleeping and attack the face in near perfect conditions. We didn't have the time. "Eiger watching" for perfect weather was out. So was yo-yoing up and down the wall in reconnaissance. We either went for it or went home.

On August 14, the day before our arrival in Grindlewald by train from Zurich, the German–Austrian super duo of Reinhold Messner and Peter Habeler had raced up the Face in ten hours in reasonable weather, climbing the wet, verglased rock and steep ice fields in record time. It was Messner's fifth trip to the wall, Habler's third. For Chris and me, it would be our first... and because of family obligations, perhaps our last. A massive low-pressure system was centered over the Berner Oberland upon our arrival. Shrouded in thick cloud, the Eiger's North Face portrayed a villain masked from those of us intent on measuring its character. Few of the Eiger's macabre landmarks could be seen.

"Isn't that lower band where Toni Kurz finally died?" I asked Chris. "Chris? Hey, man, where you going? Hey, I was just asking. Ease up, we'll be fine."

With bad weather predicted for several days, Clint Eastwood's *Eiger Sanction* production was at a standstill. The death of a cameraman and an injury to another earlier that month by rockfall far to the right side of the North Face made it imperative that weather conditions stabilize and additional safety precautions be enforced before work could proceed. It was too dangerous to film on the wall. Climbing it was another matter.

At noon on August 16, Chris and I, loaded with Eiger armor—helmets, ice hammers, crampons, and bivouac equipment—passed through Kleine Scheidegg, the small train stop and resort below the Eiger, unnoticed by the swarms of Eastwood groupies and summer

On any given day, there wasn't a better partner than Chris Kopczynski.

tourists. The telescopes on the Kleine Scheidegg Hotel's balcony were crowded with gawkers who sought climbers risking death on the Eiger's wall. A Spanish team, unbeknownst to us, was already two days up on the wall and having difficulty with the Eiger's defenses. Our climb proceeded without a stumble. Knowing rockfall was imminent in the warm, rainy weather, we scrambled to the Swallow's Nest, a two-person bivouac site named by an early pioneer, late in the afternoon. Throughout the warm night the Eiger sent us calling cards and messages of doom that whirred and exploded just beyond the protection of our rock roof. By morning, the Eiger still spoke of death, but in a frozen whisper.

"It's been nice knowing you, Chris," I said, partly in jest, then led around the corner and onto the First Ice Field.

Rocks with an apparent appetite for blood and flesh homed in on our exposed positions. I developed and perfected the loping-sprint belay, a moving target, pull-the-rope-in-when-possible belay, as the ice fields heated up.

Chris and I were Canadian Rocky Mountain rockfall veterans, but nothing short of standing beneath a dumping gravel truck could possibly have prepared us for the onslaught of rock that peppered the First, Second, and Third ice fields. Chris absorbed a ricochet on his helmet that compressed his thick wrestler's neck like a shock absorber. I danced a quick Irish jig dodging whistling death, but jagged when I should have jigged and caught a beelining, baseball-sized missile on the toe. Chouinard's book *Climbing Ice* never described the Eiger ice technique I christened "the front-point limp."

"We gotta get outta this place, if it's the last thing we ever dooooo!" I sang, as Chris leaped off the face and into the relative protection of the Death Bivouac, another one of the Eiger's descriptive landmarks of old.

Chris could only shake his head.

At the top of a steeply rising ledge system known as the Ramp, the route dead-ended below bulbous limestone overhangs. Cascading over the route was a vertical torrent thicker than a man's torso.

Lionel Terray, on his and Louie Lachenal's second ascent in 1947, encountered similar conditions. In *Borders of the Impossible,* he wrote,

"There was no doubt that this was the route, but unfortunately a heavy waterfall was foaming down it. It was in fact so heavy that we seemed likely to get washed off it if we tried to climb it."

"What the hell did Terray do, Chris?" I asked.

"I think one of them climbed the wall to the right," he guessed.

I gave the wet, crackless, slightly overhanging wall a half-hearted try, but backed off as gravity beat my already tired muscles at tug-of-war. This was not the place to break a bone.

My only option was made for my fisticuffs style of climbing. I reached through the waterfall to my elbows and found a three-inch crack hidden behind the torrent.

"Give me plenty of slack," I told Chris, "I'm not going to put in anything until I top out."

With that promise, I dived in, jamming my fists and boots like a set of pistons trying to beat the numbness diffusing rapidly from my fingers to my hands to my arms. The thirty-two degrees Fahrenheit water from the ice field above streamed through my collar and down my sleeves, soaked my shirt and pants, and filled my boots and pack.

"A tad cold to be stripped naked, isn't it?" Chris asked as he reached our bivouac ledge above and to one side of the waterfall.

"The guidebook never said anything about needing a wet suit," I replied, then continued to wring out everything but skin.

The pedestal on which we now sat, with our backs on the wall and feet dangling in space, was partially protected from the onslaught of midafternoon rockfall and on-again, off-again drizzle. I say partially, because every few minutes a rock would ricochet through the gully above, narrowly miss one or the other of us, and whir noisily into the foul and miserable night beyond the thick mist in which we now shivered uncontrollably while waiting for morning.

At daybreak, the face was coated in a glasslike, thin veneer of rime ice. Still shaking violently from our wet night on the pedestal, I stepped over Chris, checked his belay with a glance, and tackled the Ice Bulge pitch that had partially protected us throughout the night. The thin coating of ice over rock made it difficult for me to find a rhythm and warm to the effort. I bridged the gully walls above Chris and fought my way around the Ice Bulge, only to find myself on a four-hundred-foot funneled ice field steeper than the roof of a Swiss chalet and capped far above by a one-hundred-foot vertical limestone band.

"We must be off route," I yelled to Chris, still perched on our bivouac ledge. "I don't remember reading any account about an ice field above the Ramp. We're supposed to be on the Traverse of the Gods."

I could see one future write-up headline: "ROSKELLEY, KOPCZYNSKI FORGE NEW ROUTE ON EIGER NORTH FACE." But most likely, it would be written posthumously by a Swiss editor: "TWO AMERICANS LOSE ROUTE, DIE ON EIGER NORTH FACE."

I front-pointed the ever-steepening ice field to the rock band. A mangled and rusty iron piton, a survivor even if its owner wasn't, indicated to us that others had gone this way—successfully or not. I bridged, jammed, and stemmed the one-hundred-degree overhang above, finally pulling myself onto a tipped and slanted horizontal path leading across the center of the Face. We had finally reached the Traverse of the Gods, named, perhaps, for our heroes, now immortals, who had climbed such a face so many years before. Through the massive cumulus clouds a few rays of sun struck the Traverse as if those immortals were anointing Chris and me for our efforts. Our confidence returned.

I ran a rope length up an ice leg of one of the Eiger's most recognizable landmarks, the Spider. *Thunk*. A short ice axe landed in fresh snow five feet above my head.

"Hey, Kop," I yelled, "there's two guys right above me."

It was the Spanish team, dehydrated, foodless, and exhausted. I retrieved their short ice hammer and overtook them at the top of the Spider.

"*Cigaretta?*" one asked me.

Gaunt and hungry, the only treat the guy wanted was a smoke. I gave him a meat stick and led on through. I often wonder if they made the summit and down in one piece.

Above the Spider, I lay-backed Herman Buhl's verglased horror

pitch, a smooth, ball-like bump in the otherwise broken gully. I hardly noticed the difficulty as summit fever was burning through my system. A short rappel took us to the eighty-degree Exit Cracks, and three hours later Chris and I stood on the summit, embalmed in thick cloud. We were the first American team to climb the Eiger. In 1962, John Harlin, along with the German Konrad Kirch, had been the first, and only other, American to climb the North Face.

"Let's get off this pig," I said, recalling a standard joke of ours.

Chris's reply was expected. To us, a climb that was a "pig" was of the highest order. "Don't call this thing a pig until we're off it," he whispered. "We don't want to get it mad."

The descent led us down the West Flank, a maze of ice runnels, limestone pillars, and vertical cliffs. Chris had climbed the route several years before while on a summer vacation from college and knew portions of it from memory, but memory is sometimes short-lived.

The exhaustion we had experienced during the ascent dissipated quickly as adrenalin fired into our veins as each old landmark was overcome and passed. Even after two and a half days of hypothermic conditions, wet bivouacs, dodging rock bullets, and difficult climbing, we still had spark and drive on the summit.

The crunch came as we left the top. Pent-up emotions relaxed. There was no more adrenalin "lift." No motivation. Descent exhaustion crept in. Legs jellied, pack straps gnawed into our shoulders, conversation was choppy and mumbled. My boots, a half size too small, squashed my previously frostbitten toes from Dhaulagiri. If we were to err, it would be now.

Any hopes of a quick descent disappeared as we angled off-route and into loose rock and small ice slopes. Rather than risk a fall, I stopped to put on crampons. Chris rebelled at the thought, then came to his senses. Not to wear them would be a foolish mistake. He put them on.

Opposite: *John Roskelley watching for rockfall while leading the Second Icefield on the Eiger North Face, Switzerland, 1974. (Photo by Chris Kopczynski)*

The route zigzagged through short cliffs, then cut back toward the North Face above several large drop-offs. One was over a thousand feet of vertical limestone. I cramponed across a thirty-foot ice gully and turned to watch Chris.

Fatigue lined his face. The skill Chris possessed crept into his pack for a rest, and in its place appeared a beginner's error. He leaned into the thirty-degree ice slope and relaxed his hips… and slipped.

He reached ballistic velocity in an instant.

Not a sound escaped Chris's lips. The only sounds were the scraping of his crampons, his initial grunt upon hitting the ice, and the clanking of several iron pitons hanging from his pack. His face was a mask of concentration, as if he were solving a puzzle minus several pieces. Chris knew I couldn't help. He had to save himself, and there wasn't time to think, only to react.

There was nothing I could do but watch my friend die. I had always had confidence in Chris's strength and fortitude, enough so that I felt if anyone could survive a fall, Chris could. But this didn't look good. There was nowhere to stop. Nothing to hang on to.

Chris lost his ice axe the instant he attempted to ice-axe arrest. The short fifty-five-centimeter axe caught beneath him and was jerked out of his grip. He turned around to meet his fate as if perhaps he could stare it down. Sliding on his butt, hands forward, Chris tried grabbing rocks, digging in his crampons, anything he could do, which wasn't much on the steepening ice and playing card–shaped rubble.

Within seconds Chris was launched off the first cliff, a ten-footer. He tumbled into loose rock and slid. Once on his belly, Chris arched his back to dig his crampons into rock or ice. His gloved fingers clawed at the loose rock in a desperate attempt to grab anything solid.

The second cliff was not as radical. Chris flew off the edge sideways and alit on an ankle in the debris. He threw himself into a pancake position, slowed, then stopped above a thousand-foot drop.

My initial reaction was to keep watching. He was bound to start sliding again on the steep scree and rubble overlying old ice. He didn't. I realized Chris was going to live.

"Are you hurt!" I yelled.

"Just my ankle!" he replied.

"How bad?"

"Twisted, maybe sprained, but not broken!"

I glanced down toward Kleine Scheidegg, more than 5,000 vertical feet below. All thoughts of Swiss-fried steak, baked potato, and strawberry cheesecake disappeared. Chris's reply meant another cold, wet, and, this time, hungry bivouac. It began to rain.

I worked my way down toward him and picked up his ice axe on the way. He could stand and hobble, a credit to his muscular, large-boned frame, but descent would be slow and painful.

The West Flank is an exposed, embattled route caught between the horror of the Eiger's infamous North Wall, the Monch's coldness, and the icy stare of the massive Jungfrau. It's the easiest route up the Eiger, but unlike the North Wall, its treachery is subtle and hidden.

By nightfall the difficulties were above us. The mortician gray limestone of the Eiger's flank angled easily below us to the brilliant green of Swiss pasture. Cowbells echoed off the surrounding walls. We could even hear voices in Kleine Scheidegg, thousands of feet below and a mile off.

The scene wasn't grim any longer. In fact, I think a climbing buddy should twist an ankle every few years. Chris and I, after years of the kind of underlying tension only brothers and really good friends can create, got to know each other again during that unplanned bivouac. What brought us together so strongly as kids, a sharing of countless adventures, brought us together once again that night. The Eiger gave us back the humility that we had misplaced with so many successes. Our friendship, weakened through the years by competition and pride, returned with an understanding of each other's needs. Once our pride had "fallen" away on the flanks of the Eiger, we each found a lost friend.

In our youth, risk had been an acceptable form of entertainment. The greater the risk of life and limb, the more significant the adventure. What better way to test one's boldness and disregard for what life had to offer, than to keep taking risks one step further by stretching our mental and physical capabilities? Chris and I had survived the inherent risk of youth; gained skill, experience, and caution through the years; and now realized that risk was just a toy we had grown too old to use. The sport of mountaineering was now our tool for adventure and discovery.

Kleine Scheidegg, peaceful in the early dawn, sparkled as we approached it. The first few low sunbeams fired the dew on the roofs and eaves of the chalets and lit the lush green pastures. Only the milkman—a Swiss farmer driving a one-horse wagon containing old but shiny milk cans—was up and about. He tipped his hat to us in polite recognition as we passed, having seen our type many times before. Eiger climbers—crazy, but harmless.

As Chris propped his bulging ankle on the seat and looked out the window of the train bound for Grindlewald, I wondered if that dairy farmer had ever wanted to climb the Eiger.

No, I thought. He lives in the mountains. We live in the valleys. The grass is always greener....

BOURGEAU LEFT HAND

Climbing routes throughout the world, whether on the highest peaks, alpine faces, or even short, thirty-foot rock climbs, are usually christened by their original authors. Names such as Meatgrinder, a skin-ripping crack climb in Yosemite, tell a story; other names may indicate an emotion, or a time. It's the first-ascent party's reward for completing an idea, and bestows an identity upon an otherwise faceless section of rock or ice.

Bourgeau Left Hand, a seasonal frozen waterfall, had been climbed only once, by a three-man team of Canadians, Tim Auger, Rob Wood, and George Homer, in January 1974. It needed no other identity. Just designating its location in Canada's Banff National Park—Mount Bourgeau, left-hand waterfall—intimidated even the hardest Scot, Canuck, or Yank. Any other name wouldn't have done the awesome funnel of vertically hanging icicles and ribbon ice justice. Reputation alone served warning to the next party.

It was midwinter, 1975. While the Canadian alpine climbing scene was well seasoned, frozen waterfall climbing was just coming into its own. Natural-born Canadians were competing head-to-head with emigrant Scots and Brits whose winter experiences on the "Ben," Scotland's infamous cliff of mixed rock and ice, had given them the edge. Americans, for the most part, were still Yosemite-bound and tied to warm granite, two-inch cracks, and raising rock climbing's decimal system another notch.

By day, dedicated ice freaks suffered on the numerous waterfalls through minus-forty-degree temperatures, dodged falling ice, and hoped the next avalanche wouldn't sweep them off their falls. By night, back in Banff, double-fisted rounds of Labatts in the Cascade bar replaced Terrordactyl ice hammers, and talk, abetted by alcohol, warmth, and companionship, climbed a dozen more routes and much harder ones than any climbed that day.

I had climbed several of the classics, but nothing approaching a "test piece," or horror climb. More toe-dipping than diving in. My partners were usually "one-timers"—one time with Roskelley was enough. They didn't like sleeping out in temperatures that could crack glass or freezing hour after hour on some nameless waterfall that dead-ended into limestone cliffs, waiting for me to call it quits. Quitting was something I seldom did.

Jim States was different. States toughened as the weather got worse and got downright obstinate if a route roared back and tried to spit us off. Some people believe in themselves and what they can accomplish. States was one for the books.

States and I had climbed together for the first time the previous summer on the North Face of Split Peak west of Banff. Split Peak's unclimbed North Wall, a surrealistic-looking route from the highway two miles away, was on my "hit list" of challenges. As usual, I was having trouble finding a partner who wanted it as badly as I did. States, I soon found out, wanted anything with rock and ice, as long as it was outdoors and an epic.

We went after the North Face on Memorial Day, far too early in the season. In States's dented and abused tin-can canoe, we crossed the flooded Vermilion River, approached our camp below the face in knee-deep snow, then climbed the North Face of Split Peak's East Summit the next morning in freezing rain and an early summer snowstorm. States's enthusiasm, even during our ten-hour descent and hike back to camp, made me think the guy was goofy. But I'd finally found a partner who would put up with anything for adventure.

States had one fault as a climber—he believed totally in my ability and experience. If I thought we could climb a mountain or waterfall, Jim naturally assumed we could do it. The trouble was, we always did. Confidence kept breeding confidence. I never let on that I had my doubts at times whether we would make it.

It was easy for me to talk States into trying Bourgeau Left Hand. Neither of us had ever seen it up close and personal, and between the two of us, I had the only write-up from the first-ascent team. I hid that. No use putting the author's fears in the heart of my companion as write-ups and guidebooks naturally do.

I wanted the second ascent and first "clean" ascent of Bourgeau's highly touted drip—clean in that neither States nor I would use the "McKeith" method of attaching nylon four-step ladders to our ice tools and standing in them to climb the steep ice. The first-ascent team had used the McKeith method in the worst sections of ice. We intended to rely totally on our Terrordactyl ice hammers, crampons, and skill.

Bugs McKeith, a Scot who had emigrated to Canada, had taken the sport of waterfall ice climbing in the Rockies from infancy to adolescence in a few short winters. Bugs developed his own controversial method of attaching aid slings to his tools to climb ice otherwise impossible with the technology available. With his feet securely knotted in his aid slings, McKeith could take his time placing his hammers to climb or sink ice screws for protection. He didn't have to rely on balance or secure

John Roskelley practicing waterfall climbing in Washington while preparing for Bourgeau Left Hand in Alberta, Canada, 1980. (Photo by Joyce Roskelley)

crampon placements to move upward or the grip of a gorilla to hang on to his tools while screwing in a pin. Bugs's method was brilliant for use with the early, short-handled, stubby-picked tools, but it took much of the boldness and risk from some leads, much the same way bottled oxygen eliminates risk on K2 or Everest.

Bugs made the first ascents of several frozen waterfalls, such as Nemesis, that would have buckled the knees of Arnold Schwarzenegger's Terminator in fear. Regardless of his method, it took grapefruit-sized testicles to try the Canadian Rockies' worst icicles—either that or sheer madness. I suspected it was both. But McKeith hadn't yet climbed the "Left Hand."

"Come on, John," States said, "It's four o'clock. We've got to get started."

He was right. But the warmth of the car's heater and only three hours of sleep that night had crushed any determination and drive I had had on the trip from Spokane. As I leaned back in the car seat feigning sleep, my alter ego worked overtime to find an excuse not to go: some minor problem with my equipment or too much wind and cold. But I knew they were too lame for States. He was ready to go.

Leaving the car in the Sunshine ski area parking lot, we hustled across the creek bottom and through giant firs weaving and bobbing in the punchy wind gusts. We were soon above tree line, fighting our way through knee-deep powder snow and the climber's curse of the Northwest, a thick tangle of fifteen-foot-high slide alder. A wide open, forty-degree snowfield, overlying smooth limestone slabs, protected the base of Bourgeau. It had been swept throughout the years by millions of tons of snow and ice from the upper slopes of Mount Bourgeau, and vegetation, seemingly smarter than climbers, refused to grow there anymore. But there we were.

The thin, narrow first pitch of Bourgeau Left Hand looked grim in the low morning light, swept continuously by a coat of spindrift. The winter season was still early. A monstrous, vertical river of ice, as thick and wide as a building, had formed in the upper tiers, six hundred feet above, but the drip had frozen and thinned as rainlike drops passed from icicle to icicle in their effort to reach the ground. At the bottom where we now stood, chilled in our own sweat, potential excuses rampaging through our minds, the ice was the width of a book cover and paper thin. It had tried so hard to touch bottom—but failed. I could just reach the slowly dripping finger of ice with my longest tool.

"What do you think, John?" States asked.

I recognized the tone. States really meant to say, "This stinks. Let's hightail it back to Banff for some hot butter tarts at the bakery."

"Looks a bit thin, but let's give it a go," I replied, when I really wanted to say, "This is crazy. Let's get out of here before we're both killed. We can hit the bakery about opening time for some hot butter tarts." But ego minced my words.

Both of us were heavily loaded with bivouac and climbing gear, extra food and clothing. I knew from reading Tim Auger's article about their first ascent that it had taken them three days of climbing and two nights. Optimistically, we planned to cut that time in half, but we still needed the equipment.

I prepared for battle. Once my seat harness and helmet were secured and tight, I strapped on my crampons, placed the rack of ice screws, rock pins, and slings over my shoulder, lifted my thirty-pound pack onto my back, then tightened the wrist slings on my Terrordactyl ice hammers. States was still sorting his gear when I made my first moves.

Lightly, I tapped at the half-inch-thick ice at arm's length. The clawlike picks on my hammers scratched the surface and held. I pulled up, placing a fraction of my weight on my crampon front-points, which edged on tiny limestone wrinkles. Crampons have twelve points each, ten underneath the boot for glacier walking and low-angle ice and two curved eagle claws extending out front. On Bourgeau, we would need only the front two. As carefully and precisely as Michelangelo chipping on *David*, I once again placed my tools so as not to break off the two-inch-thick ice, which now held my 150 pounds plus gear. Just as carefully, I moved my front points onto the ice. The wafer-thin smear of ice, which was slightly detached from the rock, held, and my confidence climbed a notch.

As slowly as the ice had formed, but quickly enough to break into a sweat, I levitated upward, holding my breath as if the act would reduce my weight. The ice thickened as I climbed. Forty feet up, I placed a two-and-a-half-inch-long ice screw. It bottomed out. The screw might not hold a fall, but it would at least slow me down on my way to the bottom. Sixty feet above States, I screwed an ice pin to its head. It didn't matter to me that the entire slab would detach and take me with it. Success to that point spun that thin but strong web called hope.

The eighty-degree pitch ended 140 feet above States. His mind must have been in a tailspin while I chipped away at the verglas at the bottom, but with my success to the first belay, he whooped and hollered encouragement. I whooped back with the same enthusiasm, failing to mention that my belay pins were shaky at best and tied-off short to boot. He couldn't see them anyway.

I had broken off another five feet of ice at the bottom despite my caution. States was far short of reaching the end with his tools.

"Use your jumars, Jim," I yelled. "We don't have time to play on these lower pitches."

States understood and attached his jumars to the rope. Heavily laden with bivouac gear, he started up, easily removing the ice screws with a twist of his hand. I leaned back on one of my better belay pins and stood patiently watching the screw holding States move in the ice like a willow in the wind.

The sun had yet to filter across the Alberta plains and into the deep valleys of the Rockies when I heard the muffled *whump, whump, whump* of the Canadian National Park Service's powerful rescue and avalanche control helicopter. Then, out from behind Mount Bourgeau, the large orange bird exploded into view far overhead, sending air vibrations as weak as a heartbeat throughout the narrow canyon. It circled lower and lower over the parking lot until it was near our level on the ice, then cautiously approached. The cargo door was open and a ranger plainly visible.

"John. Jim. This is the park service," a ranger blared to us on a bullhorn. "You must descend immediately. I repeat, you must abandon the climb now. We are going to blast for avalanches on Bourgeau in one hour."

Although canned and mega-fied, then distorted by the helicopter's rotors, I recognized Tim Auger's voice. Auger, a Banff National Park ranger and climbing acquaintance, had given me a first-hand account of his team's first ascent of the Left Hand several weeks earlier. But, with that recognition, a fleeting thought crossed my mind. Would Tim go to this much trouble to keep a Yank team from making the second ascent of Bourgeau? Some climbers would. But not Tim. Not a chance. There wasn't a more honest man in the Canadian climbing scene.

Jim and I were experienced with various snow pack conditions, from deep powder to depth hoar, through years of outwitting (and being outwitted by) Mother Nature. Tim was not only giving us time to retreat, but emphasizing what we had already assumed and accepted—the slopes above the parking lot and our waterfall were loaded and prone to slide. Bourgeau Left Hand existed for one reason—to drain a plentiful supply of water from the wide-open snow basin far above our heads. Enter the National Park Service. To prevent massive avalanches in threatened ski areas and above roads, the park service periodically set off preplaced explosive charges by transmitter from a helicopter on key slopes. It wasn't the slope above Bourgeau Left Hand they wanted down, but it was a cold-sure candidate to slide from repercussions along the ridge where they would be working.

States jumared to my belay. "Do you think we can hustle up the next pitch, then hide in the caves above?"

I thought it over. States's idea had plenty of merit. We had climbed the worst pitch, and it would be a shame to give the climb up now. We had signed out and followed the park's regulations, and the rangers had never said a thing about avalanche control. Would they blast with us underneath? If I were dealing with one of the park's grizzly bears, I would probably have taken the chance. But with government bureaucracy?

"We'd better let them blast, Jim," I finally said. "We'll bail off, leave the rope, and get an early start tomorrow morning."

A climber out of Calgary, Laurie Skreslet, who later became the first

Canadian to summit Mount Everest, had spotted us climbing the first pitch. By midafternoon, word had traveled along the climbers' rope of communication that a Yank had led the thin, unprotected first pitch of the Left Hand—and with a full pack of bivouac gear, no less.

States's and my success stemmed from changing techniques and tools developed on the frozen gullies of northern Scotland. Climbing vertical frozen waterfalls probably originated as an off-season filler for bored Scottish gully climbers. After all, guys who wear kilts have to prove their mettle on a daily basis. But it wasn't until their technique matched their boldness and ice tools and crampons fit the angle of ice that climbing waterfalls such as Bourgeau was possible. While a few Americans were catching on, the Canadians, emigrant Scots, and Brits were quietly but efficiently climbing the grand prizes in the Rockies. Then from down south came two Yanks who easily climbed one of the classic waterfall pitches in the Rockies. Why? Simply because we didn't know we couldn't.

States relished survival under conditions that would make a polar bear cringe, not for the climb—that was strictly the medium of suffering—but as some sort of personal trial to purge himself of the week's daily grind as a physician. Leading horror pitches wasn't States's lot in life. Enduring timeless belays beneath showers of brittle ice and freezing in his own sweat in forty-below temperatures was his passion, and why he made the perfect partner.

I, on the other hand, had little patience to sit. My forte was moving upward, weaving a single web as determined and quick as a hungry house spider. I tolerate cold and mentally weaken watching my partners lead from a belay. It was an accepted reality among my partners that I would lead, perhaps because of my efficiency and speed, but more likely because my partners felt silently abused and intimidated any time I was on belay. I'm not sure I would ever have climbed with me.

Even earlier the next morning, States and I stormed up the lower slope and jumared our hanging rope. Despite the rangers' efforts to break loose the upper slopes, nothing had come down Bourgeau Left Hand.

We smelled success. This time the bivouac gear was left in the car. Without a heavy load, the climbing was easier and faster. States and I raced up the next two 150-foot pitches of ice. The sun, hidden by thick, moody snow clouds all weekend, won its battle and peeked through. The minus-twenty-degree air temperature rose slightly. States immediately complained of the "heat" and stripped accordingly.

The last hundred-foot pitch, a massive, vertical mouthful of hanging icicles, as sharp and daggerlike as dinosaur teeth, cast doubt on our success. Protecting the lead proved fruitless as each ice screw broke through to hollow ice. I smashed the teeth one by one, seeking firmer ice. Slowly I climbed out from within the mouth, found firm slush ice at the lip, and finally pulled myself onto the easy slope above. Despite the chill, sweat trickled from beneath my balaclava and helmet and ran down my neck. My knuckles, bruised and painful from smacking them between ice and the hammer handle, throbbed as feeling returned with the lowering of my hands below my heart and a fresh supply of warm blood.

I had managed in my thrashing to kick loose and break off with my hammers a ton of ice onto States. While locked into the throes of battle, I noticed him ducking and dodging like a prize-fighter, trying to avoid the barrage I sent his way. One tire-sized block broke loose under my feet as I went over the lip. I stopped thrashing to watch it target in on States, smash into a protruding icicle above his head, and deflect to the side. Not a word of complaint or protest escaped from his lips.

Fifty feet above the lip of the waterfall was a car-sized boulder in the center of the easy-angled slope. I broke trail through knee-deep powder snow to its base, found a crack, hammered in a baby angle rock pin, tied in, and collapsed in the snow.

The pin seemed bombproof. After years of pounding rock pins, I knew from the crescendoing ring as I drove it into the crack that it would hold a falling truck, let alone States's 180 pounds. But experience had also taught me to back up my anchors no matter how solid the first one was. After a brief rest, I slammed in an extra not-so-good three-quarter-inch angle.

To conserve time and energy, States choose to jumar through the loose, hanging icicles forming the pitch. I gave myself ten feet of slack, tied off the climbing rope, walked down to a comfortable spot in deep snow below the rock, and yelled for States to jumar.

I closed my eyes and enjoyed the serenity of the moment. We had just knocked off the second ascent, and first free ascent, of the Left Hand. A bit of Yankee pride snuck into my thoughts. I enjoyed a friendly competition with the Canadians and Scots. They were great climbers. Besides, competition raises the standards of the sport and the excellence of its participants, and, frankly, it's what drove me to climb in the first place.

The rope tightened as States put all his weight on the line. It slowly rose from the snow alongside me as it became taut to my first pin, three feet above my head and ten feet behind me.

Snap! I knew the sound of a pin pulling and the slack in the rope snapping into place from past experience. My eyes snapped opened just as fast, and my heart entered a new dimension in speed. My first anchor, supposedly a bomber pin, dangled above my face. States was hollering at me from below, wanting to know why he had just dropped ten feet at thirty-two feet per second. I think I heard him swear, which was out of character, but I dismissed it as a hearing problem.

"Everything's fine," I yelled back. "Just plant your tools quickly for a few minutes."

What else could I say?

The backup pin had held. The pin must have twisted in the crack and jammed with States's falling weight. At any rate, I wanted States off the rope and onto his tools until I placed another "bomber" or got into a belay.

If the pin hadn't held, States and I would have been credited with the first free descent of Bourgeau. Not a record one can live with easily.

I could just hear the rescue party.

"That ice sure breaks up human bones, doesn't it?" one would remark.

"Yeah. I wonder if their climb counts as a second ascent? They really didn't make it down with style," the second rescuer, a climber, would reply.

I unclipped the dangling pin, but didn't replace it. Replacing it would widen the crack, and the anchor now holding States might pull also. Rather than take that chance, I sat down, splayed my legs toward the waterfall, dug in my crampons, and yelled, "Okay, Jim, come on up!"

I wanted to add "fool!" knowing the risk he would be taking, but refrained.

States appeared at the lip after ten minutes of jumaring. The rope hadn't shown any of the usual stretching common to perlon ropes loaded with a climber's weight. When he got to the belay, he told me why. "I put in a tool every few feet on the way up to take some of the weight— just in case." Nothing foolish about States.

He tried to get me to tell him what happened. I dodged that.

"Just a little slack in the rope, Jim."

The word of our success spread through the underworld of Canadian climbing, the bars of Banff and Calgary. Our reputations grew with each swig of Labatts and they soon exceeded our abilities. But that's not all bad. States and I would be able to live on our "reps" for years to come. It certainly beats climbing on thin ice.

ONCE AGAIN, SELF-INFLICTED DOUBT, THE DISEASE OF
DISCOURAGEMENT, PROVED TO BE MORE DISABLING
AND HARDER TO OVERCOME THAN PHYSICAL INJURY.

ULI BIAHO

Blocky and angular, like a chunk of black marble
chipped and molded by Michelangelo, the six-foot-
two marine sergeant embodied his corps' credo, "The
Few, The Proud, The Marines." Even his United
States Marine Corps fatigues, called "baggies" by most
recruits, fit him like a Hong Kong suit.

"You!" he commanded, "get your feet down."
There was none of this "Please" or "Thank you." And
there didn't need to be.

I followed the direction in which his oversized
meathook was pointing. There slumped America's
premier rock climber, Ron Kauk, lying in his theater
seat, legs crossed, feet over the back of the seat before
him, waiting for the night's movie, *Warriors*, to begin.

Kauk, a Cochise look-alike with his shoulder-length, thick brown hair, kept in check with his trademark folded bandana, turned his head in slow motion and squinted at the sergeant with a glint in his dark eyes that said, "Maybe I will, maybe I won't." Then, at that same speed, he removed his feet and sat up. From my seat on the aisle, I could hear the sergeant's breath quicken, as if air were a precious commodity. His carotid arterial cords dilated to the width of a climbing rope and threatened to explode as he contemplated action. Then his eyes closed, reptilelike, as he searched his memory for another one so insolent. The sergeant hadn't seen this long-haired creep before. Not around the American Embassy compound, and certainly not in all the days he had been in charge of operating the embassy's movie theater in Islamabad. The sergeant disappeared.

Kauk went back to jostling and kidding two sixteen-year-old embassy-employee daughters sitting next to him, while I caught a full breath. That coal black marine, with muscles in his face bigger than my biceps, had me on the edge of my seat. The lights dimmed to match my loss of enthusiasm, and *Warriors* began.

The credits were still unraveling unknown actors when Kauk again raised his feet to the back of the seat before him. He hadn't even lowered into a full theater seat slouch when a rock-hard quadriceps bumped my elbow. It was the marine.

"YOUUUU! COM'ERE!" the marine bellowed. "NOWWWW!"

Kauk pointed to himself as if to say, "Little ol' me?," stood up, then crab-legged to the aisle and into the waiting grip of his accuser. Acting as if Kauk were cholera-ridden, Kim Schmitz and I squeezed into our seats and let him pass unobstructed. Despite the ruckus of New York street gangs fighting on screen, boisterously loud music, and solid oak lobby doors, the Marine Corps sergeant's earsplitting dressing down of Kauk reached the audience.

"What are you going to do?" Schmitz asked.

It is circumstances such as the one then before me that separate a true expedition leader from your classic load-carrying, mountain-climbing grunt. Should I interfere? Negotiate? Order a team attack? After all, I was leader of the American Uli Biaho Expedition, and with that came certain responsibilities.

"Nothing," I replied. "He got his butt into it, let him get his own butt out."

Schmitz grunted an affirmative. He recognized leadership when he heard it. Kauk, with a cowed appearance and, perhaps, temporary hearing loss, eventually retook his seat. His feet stayed glued to the floor.

The 1979 American Uli Biaho team of Kauk, Schmitz, Bill Forrest, and myself, a unit I hoped would mold into perfection by the sum of its four parts, arrived in Islamabad, Pakistan, as distinct individuals. Each of us had at least one thing in common—climbing—but life-styles, work ethics, and a generation gap were question marks in regard to compatibility.

I sought the best climbers for Uli Biaho. Two years earlier, five American alpinists, Dr. Jim Morrissey, Galen Rowell, Dennis Hennek, Schmitz, and myself, had been the first to climb to the summit of Great Trango Tower in the midst of the Karakoram Range. As I turned to belay Morrissey to the sun-baked summit, a sabertooth-shaped peak across the Trango Glacier jolted that spot in my brain reserved for nightmares, or those "challenges" best kept to my dreams.

"Galen, what's that peak across the glacier?" I asked. Rowell, one of America's best mountain photographers and a walking, breathing, mountain encyclopedia, knows the name, height, known attempts, and successful summits of every peak visible on the horizon and beyond.

"Uli Biaho," he replied. "The French attempted a route in 1976, but so far it's unclimbed."

I wasn't interested in avoiding any difficulties or following a path. I wanted the face before me, the East Face—vertical, ledgeless, yet shot with Yosemite-like crack systems. It would be a climb like El Capitan, but at altitudes up to 20,000 feet, with extreme mountain weather, zero possibility of rescue, a 4,000-foot unexplored route, and an insane,

4,000-foot approach through a 100-yard-wide glacial combat zone shot with climber-seeking missiles to Uli Biaho's rock base. Seemed reasonable to me.

Standing on the summit of Great Trango Tower after three days of struggle, Uli Biaho seemed another light-year ahead of my time. But a seed of hope fell on fertile soil—soil thick with experience, rich in desire, and at the right time in my life to foresee a destiny. Uli Biaho would feel my boots.

Uli Biaho demanded a team. T-E-A-M: A group of people organized for a particular purpose. Not a P-A-R-T-Y: A group of people out for fun and games.

Too many American expeditions organize a party and expect to put one together that works, functions, and performs. What drives me to pursue a peak or route may not drive another, equally motivated climber. Not only did I have to find three more compatible individuals to make a team of four, but each had to possess skills that, when added to those of the others, would lead to success.

I first heard of Kim Schmitz from my two-years-to-the-wiser sister, Pat. "Miss Liberal University of Washington," as I referred to her, dated Schmitz's best buddy, Jim Madsen. Schmitz and Madsen, both six-foot-plus, broad shouldered, and muscular, were stunning the California climbing locals in the late 1960s by setting speed records on Yosemite's big walls. Their team ended abruptly in 1969, when Madsen, on a false-alarm rescue, made the first free descent off the top of El Capitan. Another speed record of sorts. Schmitz overcame Madsen's untimely death and went on to set climbing standards in Yosemite Valley for another decade.

Schmitz was difficult to get to know in Yosemite, where he was a guru of sorts, but as Pat's little brother I did receive a nod or two as I endeavored to climb the "classics." In early September 1971, after earn-

Opposite: *The route up Uli Biaho ascends the narrow glacial gully below the face, then follows left of center on the spire to the snowcapped summit.*

ing my stripes on the Dihedral Wall on El Capitan and other big walls, I asked him if he wanted to climb the North American Wall.

"Nope," Schmitz declined. "I'm trying to do all my El Cap routes in two bivouacs or less."

His point was made. My Dihedral Wall partner and I had taken six days to succeed. I wasn't quite up to the guru's legacy. It didn't matter. Mead Hargis, another superb climber living in the Valley, and I flashed the climb, considered the hardest rock climb in the world at the time, in a little over two bivouacs. Schmitz no longer just nodded a greeting.

Our first climb together was on Trango Tower in 1977. Schmitz and I teamed up in the streets of Rawalpindi and bonded on the trek along the Braldu River to Trango. His habit of quiet introspection was unnerving at times, as if talk was for those who had nothing to say. If I wanted to know how to take a "Schmitzification," one of his tactless attempts to sum up a usually ridiculous situation, I would search his eyes. His large cheekbones and strong Germanic chin could have been chiseled in stone, but Schmitz's turquoise blue eyes were as easy to read as the next weather pattern in the sky. Schmitz wanted Uli Biaho.

As good as Schmitz was on big walls, I still wanted one of the younger Yosemite big-wall rock specialists on the team. There was a gang of them, like the Lost Boys in *Peter Pan*, living and breathing rock climbing all year round in the Valley, pushing vertical limits only the birds thought were possible. Ron Kauk was the best of these free-spirited athletes that only an Olympic gymnastic coach could appreciate.

To perform high-angle gymnastics on rock takes a high strength-to-weight ratio. Kauk, at 150 pounds and five feet nine inches of Jimmy Dean lean, was perfectly proportioned, plus he had the flexibility of a Labrador retriever and the grace and balance of Rudolf Nureyev. But it takes more—a lot more—to be the best. It takes the big D—Desire—and Kauk had that too.

He bouldered for hours each day; worked out in the makeshift Camp IV gym of hanging ropes, tilted boards, and balance chains; and practiced on past horror routes, while attempting and succeeding on next-to-impossible cracks. Given another athletic direction in life, Kauk could have been an Olympic champion in any sport. As it was, he lived with other Camp IV "regulars," hunted for food, bummed a buck or two, and worked part-time when convenient.

Kauk reminded me of me, except that I didn't have the guts when I was a kid to walk away from society's burdens. He did. We're raised to accept direction from our parents and society based on what's "good for you." But Kauk didn't listen. Why be another generic graduate who regurgitates generic information? He wanted the clean Yosemite air, not L.A. smog; friends who understood the freedom of rock climbing, not social clubs and lettermen sweaters; time to excel, taste adventure, and be himself.

I liked Kauk instantly. To survive year after year in Camp IV takes ingenuity, intelligence, and an easygoing attitude. Kauk had it all, plus a personality that said, "Relax, life's to enjoy, so let's have some fun." There was one enigma. Would he be there on departure day? The granite in Yosemite in June is warm and beckoning, and there's always the chance that a day's stunt work for a movie crew might come along, enough work to let him live for another year in the Valley. Was his commitment there? Schmitz was worried. And, since I didn't know Kauk, except for a brief telephone conversation, that had me worried.

"Kauk doesn't take to responsibility," Schmitz said. "We've got to find someone who will put him on the plane and organize him."

"I'll get on it," I promised, despite the impossible task. "Meanwhile it's your job to keep him pumped up."

I studied the team. It had everything—strength, experience, depth, youth.... Wait, there it was. Youth needs balance. I needed someone on the other end of the climbing spectrum. Schmitz and I would be in Nepal climbing Gaurishankar prior to making our way to Pakistan. Our two teammates would have to finish organizing the Uli Biaho Expedition in the States, then meet us in Rawalpindi. To get Kauk to Asia, on time, with expedition money and equipment, I needed someone with all our skills... plus maturity. That's a tall order in any sport. But in climbing? No way.

Then Bill Forrest came to mind. *The* Bill Forrest of Forrest Mountaineering, a profitable business. *The* Bill Forrest of the Black Canyon of the Gunnison. *The* Bill Forrest who may have introduced Fred Beckey to mountaineering. He'd been around long enough. Bill Forrest was my answer to pre-trip organization once I left the States, and the key to getting Kauk away from Yosemite, on the plane, and in Pakistan on May 31. Forrest was the only mature climber I knew who was capable, and perhaps willing, enough to go with three yahoos like us. He said yes.

F-O-R-R-E-S-T. That's how I spelled relief. I intended to have most of the expedition financed and organized before leaving with Schmitz for Gaurishankar that spring, but two months of last-minute details had to be taken care of, including getting Kauk onto the plane. Quiet, sincere, efficient, and trustworthy, Forrest was the man for the job.

I first met Bill Forrest in 1976, after my ascent of Nanda Devi in India. I was in Denver, riding the fleeting summit of success by describing heroic deeds before audiences, when the opportunity to meet the Colorado climbing legend presented itself. Not only were Forrest's ascents recognized as innovative, but his company, Forrest Mountaineering, was profitable, progressive, and competing with Chouinard's Diamond C.

Forrest's middle name should have been Easy. If I needed help contacting a corporation—he paved the way; if Kauk didn't have the right sleeping bag—Forrest got him one from his store in Denver; if our funds didn't balance—Forrest anted up out of his own pocket. With his thoughtful disposition, a smile straight out of a Roy Rogers movie, and a quiet, down-home laugh, Forrest was as easy to get along with as a meandering brook. With a profitable business like Forrest Mountaineering to his credit, Forrest was obviously sharp enough to have been in a business suit and working on Wall Street. But Forrest is his own man, and is drawn to the climber's game. I was comfortable with Forrest within minutes of meeting him—and that said it all.

Four pieces to the puzzle. Would they fit? One of the great questions in mountaineering is teamwork. What brings one group of individuals together and tears another apart? Leadership? Organization? Compatibility? As we rendezvoused in Islamabad at the home of my friend Andy

Koritko, chief security officer at the American Embassy, I couldn't find a flaw. Optimistic perhaps, but never had I felt better about a team.

After Kauk's run-in with the marine, I knew it was time to get the team out of Islamabad. Our life at the Koritkos had been a step into paradise. As head of embassy security, Andy Koritko opened the American Embassy's facilities to us, which meant cold Heinekens in a Moslem country, embassy parties, cheeseburgers, lounge chairs around the pool, and pretty bikini-clad teenyboppers who surrounded Kauk and teased him unmercifully. Kauk ignored their innuendos, flirtations, and young girl games, while Schmitz and I, sunbathing nearby, drooled over ourselves, hoping for just a moment of their time for the "old" folks. And Forrest? Well, he just wanted to get started climbing.

After eight days of negotiations with Mr. Naseer-Ullah Awan, Pakistan's head of Mountaineering and Tourism, and representatives of Pakistan International Airways (PIA, or Perhaps It Arrives), the Uli Biaho team was set to fly to Skardu in far northern Baltistan.

"What are you saying?" I asked Kauk.

"I don't like it," he replied. "There's too much rockfall."

Another squadron of rock missiles whined and bashed down the gully. Kauk and I squeezed closer together beneath a bombproof ice wall and waited for a reprieve.

"It's the time of day, Ron," I argued. "We'll start earlier tomorrow to avoid the rock. Give it a chance."

I didn't like the 100-yard-wide, 4,000-foot-high gully either. It flushed all of Uli Biaho's East Face debris onto us like a sewer pipe, but it was our only path to the wall. If I wasn't careful, Kauk would spook and quit.

"Let's cache our loads here, drop to camp, and come back tomorrow," I suggested, with more optimism than I actually felt. "It'll look better in the cool of the morning."

"Not for me," he replied, stuffing his pack with personal gear I thought we would leave.

Schmitz and Forrest were eagerly awaiting our reconnaissance report. I emphasized the great ice climbing, the protection behind the ice walls, and suggested an early-morning departure to avoid rockfall. Then Kauk spoke for the first time in hours.

"I'm not going on the route," he said. His eyes darted from the gully to us, then back to the gully. Kauk's admission put him in unfamiliar territory. I didn't speak, fearing we would lose Kauk without giving him some time to think it over.

Schmitz did. "And why not?"

"I don't like the rockfall," Kauk replied.

"Why, you big baby," Schmitz said, as if it were fact, rather than opinion. This started an all-out verbal war, Kauk screaming at Schmitz, while Schmitz, knowing he had Kauk's goat, replied evenly time after time, "You're a big man in the Valley, but you're nothing here," along with a variety of other Schmitzifications. Schmitz finally said, "We wouldn't take you anyway."

And with that, Kauk replied, as expected, "Well, I'm going, and to hell with you."

Schmitz looked over at me with a glance that said, "And that's how you handle Ron Kauk, America's rock climbing prima donna."

Forrest and I just shook our heads and continued packing—for four.

The fear within oneself too often creates mountains out of molehills. At the end of the day, Kauk let the little gremlins that feed on the unknown get the best of him again. "It's too dangerous," he said, after a long silent spell listening and watching the gully. "I'm not going."

We let it stand at that. He'd struggled with it all day and, despite Schmitz's attempt to restore Kauk's motivation with the "old boy" method, it was his decision. I knew it had taken a lot of guts to get there.

Forrest, Schmitz, and I climbed to Kauk's and my cache before dawn the next morning. Loaded with upwards of seventy pounds each, we dashed across the gully to the better-protected, higher-walled right side. Skirting large, vertical ice walls and climbing smaller seracs, we made our way to the upper ice field below the face. Intensified by the midmorning heat, rockfall ricocheted through the gully, warning us to avoid the bottleneck and seek safety along the granite walls.

Leaving Forrest to chop out a future bivouac spot, Schmitz and I donned our armor of helmets, slings, hammers, pitons, and sundry climbing gear, to test the wall's resistance. I led a quick 150 feet of ledges and cracks to a pedestal. Like the toe leather of an old shoe, the low-angled, weathered rock at the base of the wall was broken and worn, but as I climbed higher, the granite wall cleansed itself of rubble and decay and aimed for the sky in a single 4,000-foot sweep. Schmitz jumared to my stance, then led another long pitch through blocks and up short cracks.

Burdened under fifty pounds of hardware and gear as I cleaned the pitch, I leaned far to my right to surmount a block and felt a snap in my lower back, then pain.

"Time to head down, Kim," I said, as I reached his belay. "I pulled a muscle in my lower back and it won't be long before I can't walk."

By 1:30 P.M., we were down climbing the low-angled sections of ice in the gully and setting rappels over the seracs, trying to avoid the continual rock and ice fall. While beneath a series of twenty-foot-high ice blocks, two gravity-fed, climber-crushing boulders cut loose above Schmitz. He faced them squarely, defiantly, pitched one way, then dodged another as they hurtled by. Without so much as a "*whew*," or a change in the patented Schmitz muted expression, he turned down-slope and continued to descend as though avoiding a close encounter with death was on his daily job sheet.

On June 20, I stayed below on the glacier, cocked sideways, distorted by spasms, and unable to move without stabbing lower-back pain. While I lay in my sleeping bag, Forrest and Schmitz, supported by a recharged, and suddenly enthusiastic, Kauk, carried group gear partway up the gully. The team was now positioned for the final push up the gully—but I was unable to move.

Doubt within one's mind: can there be a more difficult adversary? I lay quietly absorbing the pain, watching my teammates disappear down the glacier toward base camp for food and rest, sensing an end to my dream of climbing Uli Biaho.

I'd had back problems since falling through a second-story stairwell and landing squarely on my backside while working construction in 1968. Periodically, the injury would reoccur and I would be immobile for days. But this was a first while on an expedition. With weeks of effort ahead of us—carrying massive loads and contorting in any number of strained positions day and night—could I recuperate quickly enough to continue? Would I be a burden to the team? Should I even take the chance of reinjuring my back and ending the climb for the others?

Two days later, my teammates had not returned. Out of food, irritated with their complacency, and discouraged with my injury, I limped down the glacier toward base camp. As I descended, the pain and discomfort diminished with work, and my spirit, depressed by inaction, returned. Once again, self-inflicted doubt, the disease of discouragement, proved to be more disabling and harder to overcome than physical injury. The four of us were now ready to attempt the face.

"Kim," I said, "I want you and Bill to team up. Ron and I will take the lead the first day, while you guys haul. The next day's yours."

I wanted to climb with Kauk. He was considered the best rock climber in the world. What better way for me, a self-proclaimed mountaineer, to improve my skills than to watch Kauk perform on Uli's untested walls. I was fast on rock, but with his more-recent years in the Valley, Kauk had added to his repertoire small timesavers and special techniques that I wanted to add to my climbing "tools." Furthermore, like a young puppy in a kennel with an older dog, Kauk had begun a friendly harassment of the easygoing Forrest, mostly as a time filler during dead periods of the expedition. Regardless of his intent, I didn't want his youthful exuberance to lead to a confrontation on the climb, as hunger and exhaustion fed stressed-out tempers, and the slightest added catalyst might stop the expedition in a rope length. On the other hand, Schmitz and Forrest were well matched, both in climbing and personality, and, most important, they got along.

Kauk and I leapfrogged four leads up two-inch to four-inch cracks the first day. At four o'clock, we descended to help Schmitz and Forrest haul our seven sixty-pound haul bags to our high point, a four-foot-wide ledge big enough for cooking and for two to sleep on. Kauk and I spent the night close by in our aluminum-framed hanging hammocks, called Porta-ledges. By morning, clear skies had given way to thick clouds and light snowfall.

"Oh, shit!" Kauk said, early on the morning of the 25th. "Schmitz, you got kerosene in the pot."

"It's in the water bottles we filled last night, too," Forrest added, sniffing his container.

There was no more ice on the tiny ledge for more water. None of us wanted to drink kerosene-tainted water, so we dumped it out. It would be a dry day until evening, when we could melt ice at our next camp.

As Schmitz and Forrest began leading new pitches, Kauk and I repacked the haul bags, adjusted the weight of each evenly, then began the tedious, backbreaking work of hauling them up the wall. Isolated rock and ice falling from thousands of feet above spit and cracked on the wall around us. Yells from Schmitz and Forrest warned us of the biggest or closest impending missiles.

On the third day, Kauk and I led parallel crack systems, penduluming into alternate cracks to avoid running water. Forrest and Schmitz, having fine-tuned their haul system by trial and error, moved quickly enough to catch me cleaning one of Kauk's long, difficult pitches. At mid-afternoon, I reached a seventy-degree, forty-foot-high ice field in the shape of a flying bat, the only obvious landmark we had pinpointed earlier on the featureless East Face from the glacier far below. Ice debris and small rocks showered the haul team, as Kauk led one more short, hundred-foot pitch above the ice field. Schmitz's raucous verbal abuse of Kauk's ancestry, and the real danger of cutting loose an executioner block onto Schmitz, brought Kauk back to my belay and our night's bivouac.

Fluid intake is the single most important factor in preventing health problems at high altitudes and while undertaking physically strenuous activity. Our lack of water the previous day almost proved disastrous.

Dehydrated, no one slept peacefully on Bat Ledge at 18,000 feet. Kauk and I hung in our hammocks above our teammates, who were sleeping on narrow ice platforms that had been excavated after hours of labor. Forrest, puffy in the face, lethargic, and nauseous, was obviously showing the early signs of high altitude disease.

While Forrest rested and hydrated at the bivouac site the next morning, Schmitz, Kauk, and I led and fixed 450 feet of rope. Schmitz led the crux, an overhanging gully stuffed with loose debris, that had Kauk and me cowering on the open wall, dodging death blocks, and wondering if Uli Biaho—or, for that matter, any peak—was worth the risk. At each belay, our conversation turned to Forrest. It was my responsibility, as leader, to see that everyone returned alive and well. If Forrest didn't improve by the next morning, Uli Biaho would take second place to safely evacuating Forrest to base camp.

I expected to begin evacuating Forrest on the morning of June 28, if there was no indication he had improved during the night. To continue to a higher altitude would sentence him to death if he was suffering from high altitude disease.

"How ya' feeling, Bill?" I asked, as I started the stove.

Bill opened his tightly drawn sleeping bag hood, then peered out over the Karakoram Range as if seeing it for the first time. "A lot better," he replied. "Nausea's gone and I feel a lot stronger."

He looked better. His edema, a characteristic sign of fluid retention that had all but closed his eyes the day before, was gone. Before me was the Bill Forrest I knew—enthusiastic, energetic, determined.

Decisions are never clear-cut. Just when I think I've got the situation under control and I've made my decision, a gray area appears. In this case, Forrest seemed to have recuperated.

But questions still remained. Would he worsen as we went higher, a typical scenario for high altitude–related diseases? Could a three-man team evacuate an unconscious Forrest from a higher elevation or a more difficult situation? Forrest helped us make the decision. "I'll let you know if I begin to feel worse, but we can't give up now."

Kim Schmitz, Ron Kauk, and Bill Forrest setting hammocks above the Bat Ledge snowfield, Uli Biaho, Pakistan, 1979.

"All right," I agreed. "But, Bill, you will have to jumar behind us and without a load. I don't want you working at all."

As the morning sun heated our camp, we packed quickly, then began hauling our bags up the four fixed ropes above us. After days of working together, not a moment was lost to wasted effort, nor an extra calorie spent on needless work.

The obvious crack system and deep open book we had followed up the left side of the East Face for days ended abruptly as our route and the southeast corner met. We continued on a vertical granite desert of discontinuous cracks, elephant-ear flakes, and small roofs.

At the fifth roped pitch above Bat Ledge, Schmitz and Forrest stopped to set up our four hammocks under a four-foot-wide roof. Kauk and I, released from the slow, monotonous drudgery of hauling bags and carrying packs, enjoyed two more long leads of effortless direct aid up round-edged cracks. At the end of the second lead, the summit block, an ugly assortment of icy ramparts, impossible-looking overhangs, and deep chimneys, was visible far above, but in another space and time. The hardest climbing was obviously yet to come.

We stashed the hardware at our high point and descended to the aerie built by Schmitz and Forrest, four brightly colored Porta-ledges stacked in cliff swallow–fashion on the slightly overhanging wall. Our view stretched from Paiyu Peak to the southwest to Masherbrum to the southeast, with the second-highest mountain on earth, K2, dominating the skyline to the northeast. In addition, innumerable other peaks, snakelike glaciers, and unexplored canyons highlighted the panorama and filled our senses.

The wisps of mare's tails that had sped westward throughout the day as we climbed were pursued by peak-eating cumulonimbus clouds, which trapped the day's heat like a billowy comforter. I lay sweating on my hammock and watched as each peak was gobbled up by the approaching storm. By 3:00 A.M., a cold front had arrived and wet snow had begun to fall, blanketing the cool rock and forming puddles of water in the low points of our hammocks.

The windless, mild-mannered storm drifted slowly through the

Karakoram throughout the morning. Rather than risk hypothermia while exposed on the wall, we chose to spend the next day resting out of the weather in our bivouac. By midmorning, the four of us had dug out our hammock covers and secured them in place. We now had some protection from snowfall, dripping wall water, small ice and rock debris, and the intensifying wind. Water, a precious and rare commodity on the wall below, trickled down the granite, along our anchors, and onto the hammock webbing, to eventually soak our sleeping bags, clothing, and everything attached to the wall.

I wrote in my diary, on June 29:

> I'm sometimes confused as to what I'm doing here, looking out at miles of rock and glacier, walls of ice, [and] peaks of unsurpassed beauty. Sitting on small ledges, or standing in slings, checking anchors and ropes, double checking, trusting my life to three others. Beating my hands in cracks—cold, swollen, bleeding and sore. Deadly rockfall and continuous ice. Where will it end, and for what purpose do I keep at it? Have you ever heard the whir of instant death whisk by on wings of fear? Rocks can speak, but you must always manage to hear them from beginning to end. Never break their sentence. One of the reasons I climb so hard, is so I can get above anything that can fall.

"My sleeping bag!" Schmitz, a putzer first-class, one who seems to move himself and other things continuously without purpose, yelled in frustration.

I peered, orb-eyed, out the slit in my hammock cover, through the snowstorm, and down at Schmitz. Fifty feet below him, hung up on the only ledge for 2,000 feet, a short, narrow step with a rock hook, was his sleeping bag. A teasing breeze swung it back and forth along the wall, threatening to steal it forever from Schmitz. Moving faster than I thought possible, he set up a rappel line and dropped to his bag before the breeze grew to a wind. He stopped his infernal putzing after that.

We climbed higher on June 30, but not by much. Wet clothes, cold temperatures, and thick clouds dampened our enthusiasm and made it difficult to quicken our pace. Kauk and I, haul-bag boys for the day, waited in the insufferable chill, dodging debris set loose by Schmitz and Forrest. The thin, iced cracks proved difficult. Eight hours and three hundred feet higher, they rappeled to our night's hanging bivouac.

Despite another storm approaching from Skardu, Kauk and I hauled gear to Schmitz's high point the following morning. He had led a partial pitch before abandoning the overhanging, iced-up crack system and descending to our bivouac. I continued from his last piton, zippering up the hairline crack with knife blades and tied-off ice screws. I was in a devil-take-all mood, the kind of attitude I needed to abandon my fears and charge forward regardless of the outcome.

Kauk exposed the team's melodramatic foolishness as it surfaced, with a macabre sense of humor straight from *The Far Side*. There were no sacred cows. The continual storms, dehydration, our cracked and bleeding hands, granola three times a day, iced-up cracks, sleepless nights, stuck haul bags, Schmitz's putzing, even Forrest's illness, were fodder for laughter. I knew when one of Kauk's poignant jokes had hit Schmitz: his eyes would begin to sparkle, then the lines in his usually somber expression would lighten, until, as hard as he tried not to, a smile cracked upon his lips. For a few hours, Uli Biaho was not so dangerous—death not so close.

Ron led one hundred feet to a bivouac site, a crackless, sloping bulge that looked safer than the prospects above. While Schmitz and Forrest drilled holes for bolt anchors, Ron and I fixed another three hundred feet of rope up an open book and gully system. We were now back on the East Face and six hundred feet below the summit ridge, a razor blade of rock crowned with house-sized ice mushrooms. A light snow fell as we rappeled to the worst hanging bivouac of the trip, cooked and rehydrated, and talked of the end in sight.

We went for the summit on July 2. I awoke at 4:00 A.M., hydrated the crew, then set off up two fixed lines at 7:30 A.M. It was my lead from the top of the ropes. We were below a ninety-five-degree wall, forty feet wide, enclosed by vertical side walls. A crack broke the joint of each corner.

I tried the right corner along a rotten and loose flaked chimney. It was too dangerous. I retreated and traversed left along snow, ice, and rock behind a detached flake of granite, then up a body-wide squeeze chimney. Schmitz seconded the pitch, reached my anchors, then aided an easy sixty-foot crack to an overhang. My next lead was easy aid, and I was soon on a good ledge, followed closely by the team.

"Ron," I said, "the ugliness above is *your* bag. It's all yours."

A skin-eating, five-and-a-half-inch crack, deep in the corner we had been following, leaned slightly over us. It was past noon when Kauk moved off the ledge and began engineering a path up the off-width crack with bong pitons stacked back to back, sideways, and any way that would hold his weight. Kauk couldn't seem to find any of his humor on this pitch. He ended it short below another leaning off-width five-inch crack.

Schmitz finished off the five-inch, A3 section, without a word. I jumared and cleaned the pitch to his belay. It was my turn to lead again.

I free-climbed over several chockstones, then aided a perfect one- to two-inch crack, until it flared to four inches. As soon as the four-inch crack widened, I changed cracks, aiding one that narrowed to three inches and smaller. My pitch had everything. After aiding a one-inch crack in a V-shaped corner, I chimneyed a crack the width of my helmet with no protection to an alcove beneath an ice block clogging the ever-widening chimney.

It was 6:00 P.M. Kauk, and then Schmitz, reached my stance. We were a pitch below the ice-mushroomed ridge and a long way from the summit.

"Kim," I said, "we can't spend the night out. Let's fix the three worst pitches, go back down to our bivy, then try again for the top tomorrow."

Schmitz reluctantly agreed. After not summiting on Gaurishankar, he wanted the summit of Uli at any cost and was willing to bivouac without gear to get it. Kauk, on the other hand, was not about to risk his neck beyond his norm for Uli Biaho. In fact, his discomfort had turned to anger. As far as Kauk was concerned, the icy ramparts above, the cold, and our late predicament were all preludes to disaster. I sensed an oncoming rebellion and, accordingly, made the decision to descend.

Forrest, a pitch below, was as ready and willing to bivouac as Schmitz, but trusted my judgment. Guided by starlight, we arrived at our bivouac late in the evening.

Thoughts of defeat filled my mind as I tried to sleep. Each of us had to have them. The route had turned from a clean, open wall with perfect cracks to an ugly assortment of gigantic stacked blocks, webbed together with rock-hard gray ice and crowned with immense umbrellalike cornices. The summit, well protected by battlements of rock and ice, was hidden somewhere above these monstrous cornices. Conceivably, some feature on the ridge could stop us short of the summit. It had happened on one peak or another to all of us during our years in the mountains. Without knowing what was above us, defeat snuck its way into our thoughts, like the thick, rising mist, until exhaustion kept it at bay.

By 7:00 A.M. we were on the move, jumaring to our high point. As Kauk got into a bombproof belay, I surveyed the ice plug blocking the chimney above me. It was my kind of terrain—a mountaineer's terrain—rock flakes, snow hummocks, icy cracks, and overhangs, known appropriately to mountaineers as mixed alpine shit.

I nailed a flake on the right side of the chimney, then crab-legged left underneath the ice plug. Kauk, directly below me, became a target for all the falling debris displaced by my thrashing as I struggled to gain altitude.

The one-ton ice plug that blocked my way was loose. Using my ice hammer sparingly, I chimneyed between it and the rock wall, finally reaching high enough to chop its left side away enough to crawl on top. Once past the ice plug, I surmounted one more chockstone on the ridge before pussyfooting along a sugar snow ledge to the safety of a rock cavern. Kauk, freezing from the snow that had cascaded down upon him while he was sitting in the morning chill, cleaned the pitch slowly, bringing with him my crampons and camera.

I led off again, surmounting a seventy-five-degree snow bump to steep ice steps on the left side of the ridge. One hundred and forty feet from Ron, I reached a sharp corner above a vertical, sixty-foot-wide chimney and set up my belay. Eighty feet above me on the crest of the knife-edged ridge, and leaning in my direction, was a mushroom of ice that resembled a great blue whale sounding from the deep, with its tail down-ridge and its nose against the summit wall. It must have weighed three hundred tons. There was daylight underneath its belly, and, as much as I hated the thought, that keyhole looked like the quickest route to the top.

Kauk, jumaring the rope, reached my side. He apparently didn't realize the danger of the ice perched above us, so I asked for a belay and began front-pointing up the sixty-degree ice slope. I hadn't gone far, when I swung my single ice hammer into the blue ice and a ten-pound block broke loose, but temporarily stayed put.

"Watch this block, Ron," I warned, as I continued. "It could go anytime."

As if on cue, my rope caught on the block's edge and knocked it loose. I yelled. Ron ducked, but the block, as if seeking human flesh, hit him squarely on the arm.

He cradled the arm, leaned into the rock, and moaned.

"Is it broken, Ron?" I yelled down to him. So close were we climbing on the edge of control, I feared a disaster was now about to unfold.

"That's it," he yelled back, obviously scared and angry. "I'm going down."

I could deal with an attitude problem, but a broken arm was something else altogether. Balanced on steep ice squarely beneath the whalelike ice mushroom, I was not in a position to sit tight and wait for Kauk to make a decision to climb. I gave him a few minutes to regain his composure, then asked him to finish belaying me to the keyhole beneath the ice mushroom. Robotically, he did so, angrily cussing away at his pain and our fragile predicament.

Then Schmitz arrived at Kauk's side. A discussion ensued.

"Whaddaya mean, you're going down," Schmitz asked, in a tone he reserves for lower life. "So you got hit. It's not broken. I was right, you're nothing but a big baby."

And, so it was that Kauk came next, probably to get away from all the Schmitzifications pouring from Kim.

While Schmitz and Kauk yelled at each other below, I had them tie another rope to the first, allowing me to lead through the keyhole and up a seventy-degree ice slope to avoid belaying under the mushroom. Within a few minutes I had traversed back over them and onto the last summit ridge. Once Kauk had reached my side, I led a low-angled snow pitch, the first easy pitch on the climb, to the top of the gully and into the setting sun.

A short walk and an easy slope away was the snowcapped summit. One by one, each of us climbed to its broad top, soaked in the evening's warmth, cried a little, laughed a lot, and, for just a few brief moments, forgot about the cold, thirst, and danger below.

Fifteen minutes on the summit and it was time to go. For the next two and a half days, we rappeled, lowered haul bags, and retreated. There were unavoidable incidents, close calls, bad bivouacs, and flared tempers, but as one we reached the bottom and the horizontal world we're used to calling home.

I often ask myself what the key to success was on Uli Biaho. God knows, success like ours doesn't happen every expedition. It was the team.

Putting aside my leadership, our goal, the route, the weather, and the dozens of other elements that make up an expedition, the players are what make or break the game. Schmitz, Forrest, Kauk, and I came together, body and soul, for one brief moment in time—and succeeded. Another time, another place, or a different team member, and Uli Biaho would still be a dream, instead of a memory.

YET, AS DESPERATE AS I WAS FOR REST, I KNEW I
WOULD SLEEP FOREVER IF MY EYES WERE TO CLOSE AND
THAT MEANDERING CREEK WERE EVER TO REAPPEAR.

FOUR AGAINST MAKALU

I sat up carefully so as not to disturb the stalactites of
hoarfrost that coated the tent's ceiling. It made little
difference. Little starbursts of ice crystals showered
down upon the three of us crammed into our two-man
tent. Jim States and Chris Kopczynski, my tentmates,
buried themselves deeper into their bags and held on
to their momentary thoughts of home and warmth.

"What's going on?" Chris asked.

"It's 11:30," I whispered. My voice seemed misplaced in the frosty silence. "I'm going to start cooking.
We need to leave the tent by 2:00."

There was no reply except the rustling of frozen
nylon, then silence. I fumbled for my headlamp, found

it tucked alongside the icy tent wall, and flipped the switch.

I was within a frozen tomb with two immense green larvalike cocoons alongside me. States, his intuition like that of a starling heading south for the winter, slowly tucked the tail of his cocoon beneath him, leaving a space at the doorway for me to start the MSR kerosene stove. I moved again and unintentionally broke loose another burst of ice from the ceiling.

We had carried a new stove, still in its original package, to Camp V, our high camp. As Himalayan veterans, we should have tested the stove before depending on it, but we failed to do so. The pump was defective. It would not hold pressure, and it had taken hours just to melt ice for hydrating and cooking the night before. We discussed methods of slowly torturing the individual at the factory who was responsible for quality control. I was deviant enough to be put in charge.

But that pleasure would have to wait. I started the stove, grabbed Chris Kopczynski's heavy size $12^1/2$ boot, and placed it against the pump handle to keep it inserted. This seemed to hold some pressure. My last act before again seeking the warmth of my bag was to dump ice into the pot and balance it precariously on the stove. I could now enjoy a few minutes' respite.

"Do you think we should rest today and try tomorrow?" Jim mumbled from deep within his bag.

I inched the door zipper down several inches, forced a weary 20/200 eye to the door, and focused as best I could without my glasses on the night sky.

"No. It's clear and windless. Let's go."

There was no further discussion. My experience and judgment had been under careful scrutiny throughout the pre-monsoon season of 1980, while I was leading my three teammates, Jim States, Chris Kopczynski, and Kim Momb, up Makalu's West Pillar. I had passed an ongoing rigorous test by three experts whose lives hung in the balance.

By one o'clock each of us was contorting in some slothlike movement, trying to dress without releasing more ice from the tent's walls. It was impossible. At 25,500 feet, the effort seemed to be at the limit of

Jim States ferrying a load along the West Ridge to Camp II, Makalu, Nepal Himalaya, 1980.

our stamina. We were exhausted, and hadn't even left the tent for the last 2,300 feet of climbing to Makalu's 27,800-foot summit.

Despite the nose-biting, minus-thirty-degree temperature outside, the airtight North Face VE-24 dome resembled a cold, wet sauna inside. Headlight beams punctured our foggy breath, lighting up shoelaces and zippers, cups and gloves, wherever the dark and an altitude-induced memory lapse hid our equipment.

"Have you seen my harness?"

"No. Have you seen my glove?"

Minutes after 2:00 A.M., I crawled from the tent.

The high-pitched squeak of my boots on centuries-old ice pinpointed my movements to States and Kopczynski as I fumbled with my crampons. States followed me into the night a minute later, then Kopczynski.

The bitter cold stabbed at our exposed flesh like the pick of an ice axe. Doubts surfaced, and the always-present second thoughts waged a battle within me to either return to the warmth and safety of the tent or set forth into the cold and unknown. I needed the security of enclosure. Despite the darkness, I felt vulnerable and lost in the immensity of earth and sky. But while my mind fought to restrain fears exaggerated by the unknown, I continued to put on crampons, and then uncoiled the rope. I knew that if I spilled one word of doubt at that moment when we were all so vulnerable, the three of us would retreat to the tent until morning light and then scuttle down the ropes for the lower camps, justifying each foot of descent as we ran away. None of us would really come to grips with our true reason for failure.

There was very little conversation. Our lives were linked along the rope, seventy-five feet apart, but our minds were as one. After years of climbing together throughout the world, States, Kopczynski, and I worked together like actors in a long-running Broadway play being taken on the road: the script was the same—only the stage was different.

I led off the tent platform, seeking some sort of route to follow. My headlamp narrowed my perspective; it was like looking through a microscope and searching for bacteria. I sought a simple route, but the fifty-degree ice slope narrowed and steepened and was peppered with exposed granite. A tug on the rope after seventy-five feet told me States was not ready. An "Okay!" sent me on my way again. I traversed into a steep shallow gully that shot straight above me into the stars. When in doubt, climb upward.

The self-doubt that had clouded my senses earlier disappeared with labor. I locked onto a rhythm—step, relax, breathe, breathe, breathe, step, relax.... The névé snow provided arch-deep foot placements and seemed secure from avalanche danger. We began to make headway. Where, I could not tell. But we were gaining altitude.

Once into my rhythm, I lost myself in a wild scenario that had pervaded my thoughts over the past forty-five days while I ferried loads between camps. Prior to leaving for Makalu, I had gone to see the Academy Award–winning movie *The Deer Hunter*, which dealt with the Vietnam War. The risk and stress on our troops paralleled that of Himalayan climbing. Even the sounds of choppers and the smell of gunfire resembled blasts of wind along the ridge and rockfall in the gullies.

I was never physically in Vietnam, but I imagined that I was fighting Viet Cong on Makalu's West Ridge—in the coldest, most wind-ripped white jungle ever stalked by a soldier of misfortune. It was a way to escape my own battle against Makalu. The battles I waged in the steaming jungles of my mind transported me away from the bitter cold, the heavy loads, and the loneliness of miles of rope along the West Ridge.

As I ferried load after load along the serrated edge of the West Ridge between Camp I and Camp II, I imagined formations of Hueys hugging the treetops, seeking to rescue me amidst a battalion of Viet Cong. There were days I could not recall a single step between camps—except that I had dodged a hundred bullets and missed a dozen mines. To this day, it was the only war I ever fought on a peak.

I missed Vietnam. I was drafted in the spring of 1970, but a back injury gave me a 1-Y classification—physical disability. The army's decision to pass me over didn't help my ego. In fact, physically I was as strong as I was before the accident, if not stronger, and I had no deep-rooted feelings against the war, unlike so many of my generation. The army's reluctance to take me, though, allowed me to finish college and focus my energy on climbing. To this day, I feel as though I missed an important event in my generation, but I know I would not have gone on to climb among the world's highest peaks if my energy had been diverted to war at that time in my life.

A whisper of light appeared and grew. Dark, unrecognizable shapes began to take on texture and life. States and Kopczynski were no longer just pinpoints of wavering light, but moving features of subdued color. I stopped on a wide shelf big enough for the three of us. Above rose a steep slope of granite blocks crisscrossed by gullies of ice.

We were climbing roped, but unbelayed. My mind sounded a warning. Should we belay? Climb unroped? A slip by anyone and all three of us would take an 8,000-foot plunge off the unclimbed West Face. Yet, time was critical. We could only afford to belay in extremely risky areas. The rope, though it was dangerous to climb with unbelayed, provided a link, an emotional bond with each other despite the distance apart. I decided to trust my partners implicitly and go with the bond.

Everest, so long a massive shadow twelve miles away on the western horizon, suddenly was crowned by a fiery sunrise that had traveled the length of eastern Tibet. Our seat at this meeting of two great entities in our universe would never be equalled.

At the stance, headlamps were turned off, batteries taken out and secured. Each of us sought a bit of nourishment, but because of our haste that morning, only a few candy bars and licorice bits were in our packs. We took a swig of cold water, then stored our bottles.

My feet were numb. Several days earlier, when Kopczynski and I had fixed ropes to Camp V, my feet had been so painfully cold that I had stopped, removed my boots and socks on a small ice shelf, and stuck my frozen toes on Kopczynski's warm belly flesh. It had helped and we had gone on to overcome the technical difficulties en route to our last camp. This morning, neoprene overboots were helping to protect my toes from severe frostbite. I didn't want to lose any more toes.

After forty-five days of pushing our bodies, there was little in reserve for rebellious muscles that needed rest and nourishment. A day off would have helped, even a decent night's sleep, but we didn't have that luxury. We could only think that this was it—if we reached the summit, it would be downhill clear to Kathmandu and home. Our sore throats would heal, oxygen-starved muscles would strengthen, and our world would no longer be just rock and ice, but trees, birds, insects, and warmth.

The West Ridge finally butted into the long knife-bladed Southeast Ridge. After a hundred low-angle yards, we collapsed onto the comparatively wide shoulder below the last obstacle—a five-hundred-foot-tall rock and snow summit pyramid.

After ten hours of exhausting labor, we were poised for the final push. Kopczynski volunteered to lead around the pyramid to the northeast snow slope, which we judged to be our only alternative. The western granite wall was too steep and technical, while the buttress head on would be impossible in our weakened condition. After ten hours, I was only too glad to give up the arduous task of breaking trail.

Kopczynski moved his big-boned, gaunt frame down off the Southeast Ridge into a gully of deep snow, then traversed to the east slope of the buttress. Creating a waist-deep furrow, he plowed his way slowly for ninety horizontal feet until there was nothing except snow between himself and the top of the buttress. But Chris's effort of trail busting at 27,300 feet had defeated even his world-class wrestler's muscles.

"It's useless," Chris yelled back to Jim and me. "The snow's too deep. I'm coming back."

I thought briefly of taking the lead again, but after watching Chris struggle I knew that my efforts would also be in vain. Jim and I turned and climbed back to the top of the Southeast Ridge.

There are times when a leader has to make decisions that have consequences concerning life and death. I felt that this moment was one of those times. It was 1:30 P.M., almost twelve hours since we had started. States, as tough and strong as any man, was showing signs of intense fatigue. His motor skills were impaired and his speech was slurred. Mentally, he wanted to continue. He told me so.

Examining the steep granite buttress above, I knew that States would have to be belayed all the way to the summit. He had been slow to this point. He would be even slower on the tricky terrain above. The ascent was going to take time. Time was what we didn't have if we were to descend to the safety of Camp V before dark.

"Jim, I don't think you should go on from here," I said. "You would endanger us all."

He accepted my evaluation emotionally. With tears in his eyes and his voice unrecognizable, he agreed.

Chris was a different story. I had climbed with Chris from day one of my climbing career. Physically and mentally, we resembled the famous French climbing team of Lionel Terray and Louis Lachenal. Chris was bull-like, heavily muscled, a level-headed trail buster like Terray. I was more like Lachenal—technical; a spider weaving his web up vertical planes, coolly calculating chances for success, then throwing caution to the wind and pushing forward. I was the gymnast, Chris the wrestler.

Kopczynski was staring at the buttress when I turned toward him.

"What are the chances of getting down before dark?" he asked.

"Little to none."

"I thought so," he replied. "We're not prepared to bivouac."

"No, but we could survive."

"What do you think?" he asked.

"I'm going."

Chris's level head prevailed. "I don't want to lose my fingers and toes, perhaps my life. It would be faster if you went alone. You might make it down before dark. I'll start down with Jim."

I wanted Chris's strength and companionship, but I knew he was right. Moving alone, one man might make the summit and retreat to Camp V before dark. After years of preparation and effort, the expedition had come down to five hundred vertical feet and one man.

It was not easy to separate myself from my friends. I had to do it

Opposite: *John Roskelley leading mixed ground at 24,000 feet on Makalu, Nepal Himalaya, 1980. (Photo by Chris Kopczynski)*

quickly or not at all. My herd instinct told me to descend, save myself, and forget the summit.

But there is an intensity within me that rebels against common sense—and justifiably so. I'm not in the sport of mountaineering to save myself from every potential disaster. Mountaineering demands risk. All I can do is to prepare for it the best I can, accept it, overcome it, and learn from it. There is always more than one route to your goal, and sometimes you have to let the risks justify the means. Any time I get into an intense situation, I tell myself I was given this life for nothing, so there's really nothing to lose. Sometimes it works; sometimes self-preservation wins.

This time it worked. We said our farewells. As I left, Chris yelled something about pheasant hunting in the fall, while States's final wave hurt me deep inside. They didn't expect to see me again.

As my companions began their descent, I focused my attention on the shattered granite wall above. I traversed along the spiny ice ridge until I was over the massive void of the West Face, then began tiptoeing up and left along a sharply rising left-leaning six-inch-wide ramp. The holds were sharp and protruding, which allowed me to continue to use heavy Dachstein mitts to climb. The ramp ended.

If I could angle up and right to the descending snow ridge, I would avoid a long, steep rock climb where an error would be fatal. I grabbed a huge hold above my head and did a pull-up over the block. Several more similar moves and I was able to inch to the right, intersecting the snow ridge and the top of the buttress. An old piton with a carabiner indicated I had just climbed a previous party's rappel route.

Although the east slope to my right was not intimidating, the west wall, on my left side, dropped away to the yellow specklike tents at base camp, 10,000 feet below. I moved up the ridge slowly, more in an exhausted stupor than in control, in knee-deep snow that collapsed every few feet.

I was convinced that if the snow stayed heavy and deep I would never make it to the summit. But after 150 feet, the wall on the left side retreated outward as the ridge widened and the snow became hard and

The early morning summit push, Makalu, Nepal Himalaya, 1980.

wind-packed. My rate of ascent quickened to four and sometimes six breaths per step as I moved slightly left to avoid immense east-facing cornices.

Nothing was going to stop me now. I focused on what appeared to be the summit, and could feel an energy I hadn't felt since leaving base camp flow through my legs.

Surmounting a false summit, I disappointedly gazed at several ridges joining at an apex a hundred yards away. It was the summit. The adrenaline that had motivated me over the last hump dissipated into thin air. I sagged to the snow, laid back, and closed my eyes. Within seconds I was asleep.

I transported myself into northern Idaho, to the meadow below my favorite rock climbing area, Chimney Rock. I was lying alongside the clear, deep brook that meandered through a thick carpet of alpine grass below the granite walls. A young woman with shoulder-length blonde hair lay beside me. Naked. I couldn't see her face.

Jerking up, I uncovered my watch. Sleep was a deadly invitation. It was 3:00 P.M. If I had any hopes of reaching the summit and getting down before dark, I had to get moving.

I reached the black summit pyramid, humped over my axe for a few needed seconds of rest, then pushed into the deepening snow. I moved by playing checkers with the rock boulders and snow—avoid the snow; climb the rock for better footing. The snow firmed fifteen feet from the summit. Two steps, then one, and I collapsed to my knees. I was there. The first American to summit 27,800-foot Makalu.

It was 3:30 P.M. Clouds were filling the cavities between the three great spinal ridges that met at my feet and then jaggedly vanished into Nepal and Tibet. Like the summit of Makalu, where I now stood, Everest and Lhotse, twenty-five miles to the west, stood guard above the carpet of clouds that seemed unable to surmount these magnificent bastions of rock and ice.

I was on top, but at what price? My exhaustion was total. Before me was a difficult and dangerous descent, and with fatigue would come errors. I told myself time and time again that I must make it down alive or the expedition was a failure. A death, even after the summit, was to me no summit at all.

Lionel Terray's first ascent of Makalu up the Southwest Ridge, with a large team of French climbers, Sherpas, and bottled oxygen in 1955, had been made with almost disappointing ease. He wrote of the summit in his autobiography, *Borders of the Impossible:*

Victory must be bought at the price of suffering and effort, and the clemency of the weather combined with the progress of technique had sold us this one [Makalu] too cheaply for us to appreciate it at its true value. How far it all was from the proud ecstasy I have sometimes felt as I hauled myself on to some more modest summit after a life and death struggle.

His teammate and expedition leader, Jean Franco, indicated the same disappointment in a different article that was reprinted in Terray's autobiography:

In our hearts we felt a little bit let down. Given the perfection of our tools and the continuity of our good luck, one might even have wished for a slightly tougher adversary.

There was no such disappointment for me. I had planned the expedition to limit technology—we did not use bottled oxygen. I selected perhaps one of the world's most difficult routes on an 8,000-meter peak—the West Pillar—and confined the team to four climbers and no high-altitude Sherpas. The team's three-month struggle had been nothing less than heroic, and our victory was as sweet as any I had ever had or would ever have again.

On the summit I brought out an American flag and one from the city of Spokane and took pictures of them as well as the panorama around me. I was sharing the summit with three empty Austrian oxygen bottles, left by a previous ascent party, a bamboo wand, and a package of year-old rye crackers. Famished, I wolfed down the still fresh and crispy crackers.

Clammy sweat within my clothes sent chills throughout my body. Hypothermia was only a step away. It was time to descend.

At the first rocks, fifteen feet below the top, I pried off a black rock braided with quartz veins, stuffed it in my pack, then began my descent.

As I backed down the worst sections of the upper ridge, fear of falling kept sneaking into my thoughts to rob me of my concentration. I hated my fear. It weakened me, stealing the pride I felt on top. But I couldn't escape from it. It followed me like a junkyard dog down the ridge, clouding my decisions, making something more out of losing my life than what really mattered.

My thighs and forearms became shaky pudding as total fatigue set in, but I couldn't relax at the high cost of collapse. As I approached the top of the buttress, I had to decide whether to descend the rock wall I had climbed up or to try to slide down the steep snow slope on the east that Chris had been unable to plow through to gain the top of the buttress. Sliding down on my butt was my only viable option. My muscles were not controllable enough to down-climb the almost vertical wall on the west.

I found a spot near the rock free of cornices, sat down with my legs over the steep slope, told myself that this was the only way, and pushed off. I gained momentum quickly as my descent was hurried along with my own small avalanche. I shot through several rock bands following a narrow gully, then dropped feet first into a pocket of deep snow. The avalanche that had pushed me along came to a halt. I was on an easier-angled slope close to Chris's plowed trough at his turnaround point. Within minutes I was on the Southeast Ridge where I had left my teammates hours before.

I began a race with the setting sun. A bivouac seemed imminent, but each time I stopped for ten minutes of sleep or to contemplate a good bivouac site, I regained an exhausted consciousness. I desperately needed to sleep and flopped onto my rear every ten paces to rest. At times I felt like I was coming out of heavy anesthesia. There was little hope of retracing the morning's difficulties in the exhausted condition I was in.

Yet, as desperate as I was for rest, I knew I would sleep forever if my eyes were to close and that meandering brook were ever to reappear.

My goal was to reach a natural rock cave we had passed on the way up. No longer could I hope to reach Camp V. The sun was gone and soon the residual light playing through the thick clouds would also disappear. I felt like I was in a box and the fourth lid flap was about to close. The goal was a real one. The cave had hidden itself in my subconscious on the ascent and was now pulling me down the slope, preventing me from sitting and dying on the exposed ridge.

Within ten minutes, I reached the cavelike cavity and sprawled onto my back. I heard voices. Voices are not unusual in these circumstances— in conditions affected by stress, exhaustion, hunger, and altitude. But they were so clear, yet distant.

States. That was his voice. And Kopczynski responded. Somewhere below in the deepening twilight and thick clouds the two were discussing the route back to Camp V. The crisp, clear air transported their voices straight up the ridge.

I yelled. More than food, more than oxygen, more than sleep, I needed the sound of another human being. I was still alive and wanted them to know that.

Chris responded. "John! Is that you?"

I chuckled to myself, then broke out laughing. Who did he think it was?

That moment relieved me of all the melodrama I was creating for myself. It opened up the box and let me out. Somehow I would make it to Camp V.

The air temperature dropped with the sun. The cold and a few minutes' rest snapped me out of my complacency and awakened me again to the danger of freezing to death in my sleep. I got up, put on my pack, and stumbled downward into the dark following our ascent tracks with the isolated beam of my headlamp.

I inched down backwards, seeking slope changes with my light. Several times I just managed to stop myself from tumbling backward. I checked my ice axe strap. It was secure. If I were to fall, I would slide down the gully and out into space within seconds, but at least I had a chance with an ice axe.

I was close. Every muscle and nerve was tensed for the final few yards as I rounded a car-sized boulder and stepped into camp. It was 8:30 P.M., more than eighteen hours since we had left the safety of our tent that morning. States, Kopczynski, and I hugged and congratulated each other, not so much for our success, but for making it back to camp alive.

We made it down to Camp II the next day. We had to. The stove no longer worked and a ferocious storm had socked in Makalu throughout the night and next day. It was one of the worst wind and snow storms any of us had encountered in our many years of climbing.

I am fully convinced that if I had bivouacked that night I would have died on Makalu. I wouldn't have been the first climber to fall prey to exhaustion, and I know from the years since that I wouldn't have been the last.

*Ron Kauk mesmerizing three ▲
Balti girls from Askole with
his youthful charm and wild
good looks, 1979.*

*John Roskelley carrying a ▶
live goat across a willow twig
bridge on the way to Trango
Tower, Pakistan, 1977.
(Photo by Galen Rowell)*

◀ *Jim Morrissey, Dennis Hennek, and Kim Schmitz on the first ascent of Trango Tower, Pakistan Karakoram, 1977.*

▲ *Sunset on our camp above Helé, Nepal, 1985.*

▼ *Nepalese porters from Sedoa carrying loads over Shipton Pass on the approach to Makalu, 1980.*

◀ *Jim States carrying a load to Camp III on Makalu on a bitter cold and windy day, 1980.*

▲ *John Roskelley arriving at Camp V (25,500 feet), Makalu.(Photo by Chris Kopczynski)*

▼ *The Makalu Team, top, left to right: Chris Kopczynski, Jim States; bottom, John Roskelley, Kim Momb. (Photo by Chris Kopczynski)*

▲ *Kim Momb entertaining a crowd of Tibetans in the bazaar at Xigatse, Tibet, 1981.*

▼ *Like the Great Wall of China, the West Ridge of Everest (on the right skyline) never seems to end.*

▲ Kim Momb sledding a load to advanced base camp (20,000 feet), at the foot of the West Ridge of Everest, 1983.

◄ John Roskelley being treated for edema, Mount Everest. (Photo by Galen Rowell)

◀ *Jim Wickwire*

▼ *Jim Wickwire at 16,500 feet on Denali, 1980.
 (Photo by Stimpson Bullitt)*

AT TWENTY-FIVE, MOMB WAS A DECADE YOUNGER
THAN I, YET FAR MORE MATURE AND DEPENDABLE
THAN OTHERS WITH WHOM I'D CLIMBED.

THAT'S WHAT FRIENDS ARE FOR

Momb unzipped the North Face VE-24 tent door one last time and looked in. "I'm off. Sure you don't want to go down?"

"Yeah, I'm sure," I lied. "I'd just as soon stay up here and acclimatize."

Truth was I felt like hell. My muscles ached. Even my teeth ached. One minute I burned with fever, the next I shook with chills. It was wrong for me to stay at Camp III at 24,000 feet while my teammates descended to Camp I, but I felt so bad I rebelled at the effort of dressing and descending to 20,000 feet. I decided to stay put during the storm and beat the illness with rest.

Momb's crampons screeched a cold rebellion on the ageless blue ice outside the tent as he fastened his figure-eight to the fixed line.

"I'll be back up in one day after the storm's over," he assured me. "Take care."

I was alone.

Everest's summit, 5,000 feet above me, roared its hostility. Crowned with an ice plume miles in length, the mountain grew in rage by the hour, threatening to pluck Camp III off the West Ridge and dump me back in Xigar, the nearest Tibetan village. We had prudently avoided the flat, attractive campsite on top of the West Shoulder and set our camp on the steep, icy lee side of the ridge. Everest is known for its jet stream winds. Despite protection from direct wind blasts, the drumskin-tight walls of the VE-24 still hummed a monotonous verse of "Stormy Weather" as powerful wind rotors whipped over the ridge.

This was my second trip to Everest. And, like my first, to the East Face in 1981, it was beset with minor problems from the beginning. First, the expedition was in debt for $127,000. Our major sponsor, a television network, had dropped its support one month before our departure and given the money to a South Col Everest team. The network liked the South Col expedition's chances of success better than ours. Our expedition had decided months before departure not to take Sherpas or to use bottled oxygen. Our integrity and purity of style cost us dearly.

Second, and worse, our expedition manager, hired to organize and procure equipment, turned out to be a drug addict. He had fast-talked his way onto the team as a Tibetan scholar and translator. This problem reached a peak in Chengdu, China.

An impromptu party in the snooker room of the foreigners-only hotel ended in the wee hours of the morning. Later, the expedition manager snuck into another room and tried to stuff cocaine up several inebriated climbers' noses. The climbers awoke, still in a drunken stupor, fought him off, and put him back in his own room. Despondent, he broke a beer bottle, cut his leg, and bled on the hotel's bedding and expensive Chinese rugs.

Kim Momb and friends, Lhasa, Tibet, 1981.

The expedition members departed the hotel at 3:00 A.M. to make the flight to Lhasa, Tibet. It wasn't until we arrived at our hotel that afternoon that expedition leader Bob Craig was handed a telegram from the Chinese Mountaineering Federation director in Chengdu. He was informed officially that the expedition was responsible for the cleaning bills for sheets, bed covers, and expensive rugs soaked in blood. Furthermore, one more incident involving our team and we would be asked to leave the country immediately.

The guilty party was put on notice—one more foul-up and he would personally pay with his hide.

But the problems didn't stop there. At base camp our doctor, rummaging through the medical box, discovered that all the Percodan and codeine-related pills were missing, along with other prospective "recreational" drugs.

In a team meeting that afternoon I demanded that the "manager" be shipped out that day or, at the very least, tied and gagged until the next jeep could take him out. I was voted down simply because the manager convinced the team leaders, again, that he would behave himself. He was put on probation and watched day and night. He finally left the expedition a week later when another climber had to leave due to problems with cerebral edema. Everyone felt a bit easier with his departure.

These were minor problems compared to my own physical ones prior to and during the trip. Feeling poorly for several days before leaving the States, I took a sulfa drug called Septra in case it was a recurring bladder infection. I developed an allergic reaction.

A high-speed trip to the hospital, a shot of adrenaline, and some pills seemed to help. I went home. Several hours later I woke up unable to breathe. Without waking my wife, Joyce, I got up, dressed, and drove to the hospital again. The doctor took one look at me, stood me up against a gurney, and stabbed me in the butt with an injection of Visceral, a strong antiallergen. "This is going to hurt," I remember him saying.

Pain shot through my hip. My legs buckled and I lost consciousness.

"Must have hurt worse than I thought," the doc said as I came to on the floor.

"No shit," I muttered. Then I went back to sleep.

Around 5:00 A.M., the orderly woke me up and sent me home. Joyce was still sleeping. She never even knew I had left the house.

Several days later I was in Tibet, still weak and fighting the same illness I had taken the Septra for. Little did I know then that this problem would stay with me throughout the expedition.

So it came as no surprise to me that the fever had returned at Camp III or that I had another illness. It seems that one problem always leads to another, especially at altitude.

After three days the storm blew itself out. I felt better. My chills and fever were gone and I even began to feel energetic.

"Camp III to base," I called on the radio. "I'm going to carry to the end of the fixed ropes. Talk with you at six tonight."

"For God's sakes, Roskelley, wait for someone else!" Craig replied.

I ignored his advice and left the tent. Already the sun had warmed the still air. The Himalaya were cloudless. Pumori, Gaurishankar, Menlungtse, and other peaks—unnamed and unclimbed—burst into orange as each was hit in turn by the rays of the rising sun. Five thousand feet below, my teammates were beginning to ascend the ropes.

I reached the rounded shoulder of the West Ridge within minutes after leaving Camp III and began the arduous task of pulling out the fixed rope buried like underground cable beneath wind-packed slabs. Three-quarters of the way along the slowly rising ridge, I reached the end of the fixed lines Momb and I had placed before the storm. It was still early.

Unraveling a coil of rope from my pack, I set off along the ridge unbelayed, paying out the rope as I went. The climbing was easy and within several hours I had fixed all the rope I carried and was within one rope-length of Camp IV. This was my day, and I felt like the Roskelley of old. After spending one of my finest days in the mountains, I returned to Camp III in early afternoon.

Momb burst into Camp III like a small atomic bomb. He had just ascended the 4,000 feet of fixed lines in a matter of hours. He was exhilarated. There was no one on the team who could match Momb's strength at that moment.

Momb was my partner, and protégé—and damn proud of it. I trusted him. Believed in his judgment. At twenty-five, Momb was a decade younger than I, yet far more mature and dependable than others with whom I'd climbed. There wasn't a climb I wouldn't do with him. In fact, my insistence on taking him on the 1981 Everest Expedition had created insurmountable problems with others on the team because of his inexperience.

Momb was a first-year rock climber when we met at the Spokane Mountaineers chalet on New Year's Eve in 1978.

"Stand back," I said to myself when I first saw him. "What am I looking at?"

What I saw was the Hulk in miniature—a five-foot six-inch block of pulsating muscle. Here was a young man with thighs as big around as my torso, upper-arm development that put Arnold Schwarzenegger to shame, but with a waist smaller than mine and a bone-crushing grip. If he had an ounce of coordination and intelligence I figured right there he'd make a hell of a climber. He had both—and more.

What made Kim Momb special was his heart. There was none bigger or more caring. When we first met he had a simple creed—be the best he could be at everything.

Momb raced motocross as a kid. He was good. Good enough to race for the Yamaha factory team. Momb skied. Why he never raced for the World Cup team I'll never know, because there was not a better skier on any mountain on any given day. Momb knew karate. Lord help the guy, no matter how big and tall, who pissed him off. Momb also played the guitar and sang—not quite like Garth Brooks, but damn close.

But I noticed early on that once Momb mastered a sport, he would move on to another. He didn't need to get a gold medal or win the next race. Momb was comfortable with himself and his ability, not impressed by the hardware that accumulates with success. He was one of those rare individuals who was not afraid to fail.

I tried hard to make climbing a fun sport when we were together. I was afraid he would move on to other things and leave me searching for another partner as I had had to do so many times before with younger guys. Momb had a spirit I was comfortable with. I needed him much more than he needed me.

While I struggled to maintain my health throughout the trip, Momb's efforts to carry loads and push the expedition ahead of schedule were phenomenal. We had separated briefly after arriving at base so that I could recuperate from my illness, then teamed up again to lead pitches above Camp I to Camps II and III.

Our speed and efficiency were the talk of the team. After several days of climbing on the difficult icy buttress above Camp I, we put the expedition well ahead of schedule.

The afternoon of Momb's return to Camp III, while heating our dinners in a bag ("flight bags" as we referred to them, recognizing their similarity to vomit bags on airlines), we sang a few bars from "Sail On"

Kim Momb preparing to lead, 26,000 feet on the West Ridge of Everest, 1983.

by Lionel Richie. Momb never forgot words to songs, while I never remembered them. He would keep the tune and remind me of the lines as we went. Richie's lyrics brought back warm memories of past adventures together.

To this day I think of Momb every time ol' Lionel cranks out a tune on the radio. But I can't buy his tapes. The good-time memories would just hurt too much.

Momb and I carried loads to Camp IV at 25,000 feet the morning after his arrival. The next day, supported by Jack Tackle and Mike Graber, the two of us moved into high camp to work on the route above.

Momb and I read each other's minds continually. There was none of the usual second guessing. I knew what he was going to do next and vice versa. There was not a better team in the mountains.

Wind slab where the West Ridge met the steepening upper wall of Everest staggered my early momentum as we climbed above Camp IV the next morning. Loaded with ropes and hardware, I felt an ever-increasing lethargy. Momb felt the altitude too, struggling on the icy slope, trying in vain not to cut loose barrages of ice and loose rock.

"I sure have a funny cough, Kim," I said at a belay stance. "Do you have one?"

"Oh, yeah," he replied. "Everyone's got one. It was the shits sleeping in the big tent at base, there was so much coughing."

"Well, I never get coughs," I said.

And I didn't. Not deep, rumbling coughs like this one. I felt as though I had forgotten something and just couldn't remember what it was. There was a nagging sensation in my mind. A question, but no answer. I stopped worrying about it when the cough disappeared on the descent to Camp IV.

Dreams are fantasies, fantasies that create a world not as it really is. Hidden within dreams are bits of reality. A dog barks outside the house. The mind creates a dog within the dream. An uncomfortable lump alongside the tent wall pushes against my rib and I dream of taking a blow on the same rib in a fight protecting my kids. An alarm clock's screech becomes a train's whistle.

Deep into the night I awoke from a dream where there was running water. I heard gurgling, the movement of fluid within an enclosed container. It bothered me.

Disoriented in the dark, I found my flashlight and regained a drowsy consciousness. I leaned up on my elbow to clear my head.

"Was I dreaming?" I thought. "Was that running water? Or could that gurgling have come from my lungs?"

I took a deep breath, held it, focused all my attention within my chest for the sound of fluid, and exhaled.

I felt it first. Like spittle creeping down a dry throat. It was bumpy, as if the fluid moving through my lungs was impaired by narrow air ducts. Then the gurgling sound.

I was still in a dream state, a semiconsciousness, probably the same state that a yogi or Hindu ascetic attains in order to overcome self-inflicted pain. In this condition, I could clearly detect fluid flowing within my lungs as I breathed. Not audibly, but similar to feeling blood pounding in my head after a hard run.

I had a terrible urge to pee. Somehow I found my pee bottle and unscrewed the cap. I got to my knees with difficulty and began swaying in the dark. I missed the pee bottle. It was only then that I realized how sick I was.

"Kim, you awake?" I whispered.

"Yeah, can't you sleep?"

"I have pulmonary edema."

"You're dreaming," Momb said. "We'll take a break tomorrow and you'll feel better."

"I'm not kidding," I replied. "I can hear fluid in my lungs and I missed my pee bottle."

"Missed your pee bottle!" Momb repeated as if everything now made sense. Roskelley never missed his pee bottle.

The situation was not good. There was no bottled oxygen or medical kit in camp. Camp III was a mile away along the ridge with very little elevation drop until just above the camp. Radio call to the lower camps was not until 8:00 A.M. We could not wait for help from Camp III. I would soon lapse into a coma and perhaps die within hours waiting for rescue.

Momb melted ice and boiled water for tea while I dressed. Instantly exhaustion overwhelmed me from the exertion. As long as I lay deathly still, the disease took its time—to kill me. Physical effort accelerated the effects of the disease. Could I descend the ridge fast enough to keep from drowning in my own fluids?

Momb popped his crampons on as I crawled from the tent. I coughed. It was the same as the day before and I should have heeded the obvious sign. The cough was my prelude to disaster.

"There it is. I'm on my crampon," I thought. "Why can't I bend over and fasten it?"

Momb noticed my bewildered look, leaned over, and fastened it, realizing I was worse off than he thought. He outlined a plan of descent. He would go first, dig out the rope, and wait for me at each anchor. Could I follow?

I thought I could, but my hands and feet were cold. Almost numb. Because of the pulmonary edema, my body was shutting down blood flow to the extremities to save the core. I was drowning little by little—and still a mile to go.

I carried nothing. Every step sideways along the traverse I lurched or stumbled. I tried to follow quickly, but I was losing interest in everything around me because my brain was hypoxic due to the lack of gas exchange in my quickly flooding lungs.

Midway along the traverse I lost all feeling in my hands and feet. Momb opened his coat, removed my gloves, and shoved my stiff, colorless hands under his armpits. I was showing no emotion, a sign I was far enough gone not to care.

Momb was scared. Scared I was going to quit. Scared he would have to leave his best buddy to die on a remote, windswept hunk of rock and ice. Scared because he could see into eyes that no longer mirrored the intensity of the person inside.

Each rope took me longer to negotiate. At each anchor, Momb

would warm my hands, pump my arms, tell me to keep going, clip me into the next rope. Then tell me about Jess, my one-year-old son. About Joyce. About home and how we would mountain bike, boulder, and never come back to the Himalaya.

I listened, watching tears well in his eyes. I wanted to move, but my hands and feet would not cooperate. I wanted to feel emotion, but I no longer cared about living.

I collapsed on the shoulder of the West Ridge several hundred feet above Camp III.

"I've got to rest," I said, then lay down and closed my eyes.

"Come on! You're not done yet, Roskelley," Momb yelled.

He pulled me into a sitting position and made me open my eyes. "You're going to die if you don't get up," he said.

That was true—but I didn't care. Momb leaned back and jerked me to my feet. Grabbing me underneath my arm, he led me to the two steep ropes above Camp III, clipped my figure-eight into the rappel line, and forced me to descend.

The climbers at Camp III heard Momb yell for assistance far above camp. Climbers appeared from the two tents immediately.

Once into camp, I was taken from the rope, placed in a tent, and given water. Robin Houston, one of our team physicians, found an oxygen bottle but no regulator.

"Steve," Houston said to his tentmate, Steve McKinney, "open the bottle full tilt and let the oxygen fill the tent."

McKinney performed that task as Houston rubbed my hands in an attempt to get feeling back into them. It was useless. I had to descend much farther to stay alive.

Houston volunteered to help Momb get me down to Camp I. I was very weak and still had no feeling in my hands and feet. Within half an hour I was hooked into the fixed lines and told to descend. Momb would secure my figure-eight—Houston would follow in case I needed assistance from above.

I stumbled and fell constantly on the 2,000-vertical-foot descent to

Camp II. Feeling began to return to my hands, but with the huge mitts I was given to wear at Camp III, I was unable to manipulate my own figure-eight.

Mike Graber appeared at Camp II as the three of us rested. He must have seen the pain and exhaustion in my eyes. Without a word, Graber unzipped his coats, grabbed my icelike hands, and pressed them against his belly skin. I froze that moment of kindness in my heart. I couldn't turn my head or hide my face with my hands pulled tight to his waist. He saw the tears, and I didn't try to stop them.

Once past Camp II, I began to revive. The rales were gone. I felt like fighting to stay alive. My hands and feet were beginning to tingle. Life looked reasonable again.

We reached Camp I early that afternoon. At 20,000 feet I felt exhausted, but knew I would recuperate. The 5,000-foot descent from Camp IV had saved me. It had been my only choice.

I owe my life to Kim Momb. He kept me moving, pushed me beyond my physical limits, and wouldn't let me give up. I had seen this humanity within him years before, and it was why I climbed with him and not with so many others.

The inevitable naysayers appeared after the trip. "You'll never be able to go to altitude again," the "experts" told me. All sorts of hypotheses, precedents, and "facts" were offered up based on past studies and accident reports.

I didn't believe any of them. I couldn't. I believed then—and still do—that only I know my limitations and potential. I knew what had induced *my* pulmonary edema: prior illness. My body's immune system had been weakened from fighting an illness throughout the trip. This opened the door for the disease.

Medical science had failed me before. Physicians, the best there are, couldn't even tell me I had worms for nine months in 1978. A shoeless Nepalese lab technician found them immediately upon my return to Nepal in 1979. So when one of the most knowledgeable American physicians on high-altitude disease discounted my theory that since a prior illness had set the stage for my pulmonary edema, I could go back to altitude without a problem, I paid little attention to him.

In fact, I returned to Everest the next year, 1984, as strong and healthy as I have ever been. On that expedition, I climbed to 28,000 feet without oxygen and turned around only because of the fear I had of losing my hands and feet to frostbite from the intense cold of late October and after spending so much time at altitude.

Our 1983 West Ridge Expedition failed short of the summit. Momb was disappointed but quickly made arrangements to attempt Everest that fall from the east side. He and five others, using oxygen from their last camp, made the first ascent of Everest's East Face. Momb, once again, proved to be the strongest climber on the team.

Postscript

Kim Momb worked as a heli-ski guide during the winter months in the Interior Ranges of British Columbia. I saw him too infrequently.

It was early January, 1986, when I spoke to him last. He was in Spokane for a few days and we played racquetball one afternoon at the Spokane Club.

The Interior Ranges had a lot of snow that year—more than usual. But what bothered me was a recent change in the weather. It was warm and drizzling. The current weather and the preceding weeks of snow accumulation matched the conditions several years earlier when Willi Unsoeld was buried by an avalanche and killed on Mount Rainier.

As Momb and I walked into the rain toward our cars in the parking lot, I said good-bye. "Give me a call next time you're in town, Kim. And be careful. Avalanche conditions should be terrible this week."

Momb died two days later. He and two clients, one who also died, were swept into the trees by a slab avalanche while skiing a remote mountain slope in British Columbia.

'NOBODY COULD HAVE FALLEN LIKE THAT AND WALKED
AWAY,' I IMAGINED HIM SAYING. OR, 'MOST MEN
WOULD HAVE BLED TO DEATH,
BUT NOT JOHN ROSKELLEY.'

OL' HEREFORD

Terminal illness came to mind as my wife, Joyce, and I exited the roll-a-bed-sized elevator and entered Valley General Hospital's faded lime green third-floor waiting room. It was quiet except for an asthma sufferer's wet cough down the hall. Pine Sol invaded my nostrils, fighting and winning the daily odor battle against a selection of leftover lunches on a service tray nearby.

The waiting room looked like a full-page color ad in a Sears flyer I saw in the Sunday paper promoting brass-based lamps, wooden-armed easy chairs, and a matching couch. On the rectangular parquet oak coffee table were several large ceramic ashtrays.

John Roskelley and Will Hawkins with bull elk in northern Idaho, 1980. (Photo by Will Hawkins)

Spokane's Valley General Hospital was—in theory—a "No Smoking" hospital.

Will Hawkins's family was doing what people do in waiting rooms, mindlessly flipping through two-month-old *People* magazines, sauntering out to the drinking fountain, and occasionally picking up and unfolding any number of hospital brochures on subjects ranging from asthma to venereal disease. I detected a slight nervousness, not unlike that of a poodle in the wrong house. They were in need of solid information. So far, there was not the frightened tension and urgency that accompanies bad news.

"The doctor asked him to come in for tests," Will's wife, Joan, said. "His spasms in the lower back have been getting worse."

"A short stay in the hospital will get him on his feet again," I replied. "You know Will, Joan. He just won't let those injured muscles heal."

Will Hawkins had never been sick a day in his life until 1982, when he had been diagnosed as having testicular cancer.

Everyone expects a cold or flu. Children bring illnesses home during the school years as often as pinecones fall from a tree. But cancer at the age of forty-three?

Will's doctors felt they had caught the disease in time and were satisfied with surgery and localized radiation. Will wasn't so sure.

"I feel kind of weak," he told me before I guided him to the top of the Grand Teton two summers later, along with his son, Bill, and daughter, Nikki.

In April 1985, a year after our trip on the Grand, his back began giving him stabbing, painful spasms. At times he couldn't stand, let alone walk. Will had come to Spokane from his home in Sandpoint, Idaho, for more sophisticated tests. What bothered Will the most was he couldn't remember straining his back prior to the pain.

He hadn't. It was multiple myeloma, a deadly type of blood cancer.

September 1984

"Boy," Will Hawkins said. The "b" burst from his mouth like he was squirting a cheek full of water. He drawled the "oy" for emphasis. It was his word, like some people use "holy smoke" or "gee whiz."

"Boy," he repeated, "he was a big buck."

Will had seen a lot of big bucks. Right away, I knew this one was special.

"Picked him out across the canyon," he said. "Had a face as white as snow. Named him Ol' Hereford."

"What about Ol' Hereford's rack?" I asked. I was an antler man.

"Booooy!" he said again. "I thought he was a five-point bull elk at first. He had a spread this big."

His arms went out past his shoulders and widened. Will wasn't prone to exaggeration. Well, maybe a little.

"He was the biggest buck I've ever seen," Will said flatly.

That was big. Will had a monster mule deer hung on his wall at home. It was one of the biggest ever taken in Idaho.

At forty-five, nine years older than I, Will had killed scores of both mule and white-tailed deer. He was to hunting what Roy Hobbs in *The Natural* was to baseball: "The best there ever was and the best there ever will be."

Hunting with Will was like having a private basketball lesson from Michael Jordan or a week of climbing with Reinhold Messner. I learned something about the woods or an animal every minute. Common-sense stuff that old dogs and grampas know. Things a book just can't tell you. Will was "down-home" smart.

"Too bad it wasn't deer season," I sympathized.

"I know just where he'll be during rut," he answered. "We'll make an all-out effort to get him."

After five years of hunting with Will in northern Idaho, I knew we would chase that buck. He had put me in front of bear, elk, and deer each year since our friendship began in 1979.

Will Hawkins was born and raised on "Sunnyside," a peninsula on the west shore of Pend Oreille Lake five miles east of Sandpoint, Idaho. His father, Dal Hawkins, was raised there. So was his grandfather. Four generations of Hawkinses had logged, farmed, and lived on a section of land that God had reserved for His retirement.

The Hawkins family is a treasure, a piece of Americana. They worked hard, treated each other with respect, and stayed close to the land. So rare a treasure, in fact, that I thought they should be entered in some National Historic Register as an example of "The American Family As It Should Be."

Will's dream, his lifelong ambition, was to climb Chimney Rock, a northern Idaho landmark. He could see it from his home as he grew up. It was like marrying the girl next door. He had to do it. The idea scared him to death, but he knew his life would not be complete unless he stepped on top of that four-hundred-foot pillar of rock.

I guided him up it in the summer of 1979.

Perhaps I got more out of the experience than Will. I had climbed it twenty-five times, by every side, by most routes, but never with someone who loved that rock more than he did.

I didn't know Will then. Guiding was a job, some quick cash to tide me over because, as usual, I was broke. But by the end of the weekend I felt guilty accepting his money. He threatened that if I didn't accept it he wouldn't take me bear hunting. I pocketed the check.

My guilt for being paid wasn't only because of Will. I liked him. He was unassuming, polite, reserved. It was also because of his family and friends. They were the same way.

Knowing Will's greatest dream was to reach the top of Chimney Rock, his entire family—his wife, Joan, his son, Bill, his daughters, Mitsy and Nikki, and his dad, Dal—spent the weekend with us in the glaciated alpine meadows below "The Rock." In addition, several other relatives, friends, and a former governor of Idaho came in to watch the climb. One friend even flew over Chimney Rock in his Cessna 180 at a prearranged time. Will's mother, Teddy, waited in the pasture above the house at noon for the sun flashing off a mirror from the summit twenty-three miles away. Will wanted her, too, to know he had made it.

They did this for Will because he had given of himself time and time again for them. He had more friends than a puppy in a pet store window. Bragging-type friends. Ones who considered Will's happiness their happiness.

October 1985

I had never had a friend with cancer before. Good friends had come and gone. Many had died in mountaineering accidents. Quickly. Not having to suffer the torture of slowly disintegrating, wilting before their own eyes.

Will had been told at Valley General that his cancer was possibly terminal. Physicians always add "possibly." They've probably heard of a few miracles, though never had one happen themselves. But stories seem to live and grow in cancer wards of patients diagnosed with terminal illnesses going into complete remission and living normal lives forever, or of cures resulting from treatments not approved by the FDA but found in foreign lands where they're legal. Details are always sketchy, the treatments expensive. They keep the patient's hope alive. And, perhaps more important, the family's.

"How are you doing today, Will?" I asked, several months after his cancer was diagnosed.

"Had some bad spasms last night," he replied.

Heavily sedated with painkillers, Will slurred his words as he fought to clear his head. He had been in bed for months, unable to roll to his side or sit. I grabbed his hand and held it lightly. It was cool and moist. His skin was sallow and wrinkled and fit like a hand-me-down coat from an older brother.

The eyes that could spot a deer's browline in heavy cover wavered, then focused on mine. I remembered seeing a black-and-white photo of Will as a boy on the Sandpoint basketball team and thinking how eager and proud his eyes were. They were still the same, sparkling and alive, despite the pain and circumstances. I knew then that I loved this man like a brother.

"I might not get a chance at Ol' Hereford this year," he pondered. "But, boooy, he better watch out next year."

The disease seemed in control some days, then took off on others. Will was living at Sacred Heart Medical Center in Spokane during his radiation treatments. I was able to visit daily with my three-year-old son, Jess.

"Why does Uncle Will have to stay in the hospital, Daddy?"

"To get well, Jess," I lied.

"Why are you crying, Daddy?"

Will's heroes were mountain climbers. He knew more about Maurice Herzog, Sir Edmund Hillary, and Jim Whittaker than I did. I also knew I was his greatest hero.

That's hard to live up to. I got tired of busting through brush after deer or carrying heavy loads uphill. But I couldn't let him know it. When

I got cranky, I tried not to let him know that either. It was a full-time job trying to act perfect. I often failed. But Will always gave me an excuse and a way out. That's friendship.

I just couldn't do anything wrong in his eyes. One summer I took Will, his fifteen-year-old daughter, Nikki, and thirteen-year-old son, Bill, to the top of Mount Rainier in Washington. It's a grunt of a climb. I've had triathletes fail to summit, and some professional athletes say it was the toughest thing they've ever done. But despite never having put on crampons until the summit morning or walked on a glacier, the kids made the summit. That kind of determination always brings tears to my eyes.

I roped them up at the crater rim for the descent. Will was talking to two climbers eating lunch nearby as I finished tying Nikki to the rope.

"That's John Roskelley," I overheard him say. "Best climber in the world. Just brought us beginners up here."

They glanced in my direction.

I cringed a little, not caring to be put on a pedestal.

"Follow the track, Will," I hollered down to him. "We're right behind you."

Will started down, followed by Bill, then Nikki, then me. Earlier that morning, I had changed my crampon straps with Nikki's because of an adjustment problem on her boots. I thought it was more important that her crampons fit better than mine.

Fifty feet off the crater rim I stumbled, then crumpled like a shot duck in midstep. I was in a foot-deep ice trough created by hundreds of Rainier climbers using the same path. A front point on my left crampon caught in the loose-fitting crampon strap on the opposite boot. My momentum tossed me forward, feet locked together. I toppled steeply downhill into the icy trough like a serac dropping off an ice cliff. I hit the ice hard with my forehead and exposed forearms, sliding for ten feet before getting control.

The pain shot through my arms, shoulders, and head. Blood from ice-shredded skin quickly reddened the hard white ice. It hurt. But not as much as the disbelief Will had on his face.

"John Roskelley fell?"

I glanced at the two climbers Will had impressed just minutes before. They were still eating, but with smiles on their faces. I had just made their grunt to the top of Mount Rainier worth the trouble.

"Keep going, Will," I yelled. "Just caught a crampon. What? No, I'm not bleeding... badly. A knot? On my head? No. Doesn't hurt... much."

Will's "hero" had blundered again. But I knew he would maximize this one to my advantage.

"Nobody could have fallen like that and walked away," I imagined him saying. Or, "Most men would have bled to death, but not John Roskelley."

Will never let me down.

For taking Will up Chimney Rock I unexpectedly reaped additional rewards. I was an instant member of the Hawkins clan. I felt their thanks a million ways and they opened their hearts to me and my family. In addition, Will's friends became mine.

The responsibility was overwhelming. It was impossible to live up to. But it didn't matter. He never ceased praising my adventures, my character, and my life.

Our friendship grew as the years went by. I took Will and his kids on more climbs, and he and I hunted the beautiful Selkirk country each fall. Will and Joan became our son Jess's godparents.

It was in the fall of 1979, after our ascent of Chimney Rock, that Will displayed to me his unusual talent for hunting.

Will focused his energy on the animal and became one with his prey. He concentrated as if he were the hunted. Like a superb athlete, he eliminated all thought other than the objective—seeing the animal. Not just looking, but really *seeing*.

Will was as deadly as a heat-seeking missile, but I saw him kill only one animal—and that for food.

"I don't need to kill any more animals," he once told me. "I get more fun out of just hunting them."

Will had already put me in front of a nice black bear that September.

This trip he wanted me to shoot a big mule deer buck. Like his dream was to climb Chimney Rock, mine was getting a granddaddy mule deer.

He and his dad, Dal, had the horses and mules loaded in the truck by 5:00 A.M. The snow squeaked underfoot as I carried my gun and daypack over to the Chevy one-ton laden with their damaged and weathered homemade stock rack and four animals. The two horses and two mules were in their usual positions of head to tail. Tinkerbell, one of the Appaloosa mules, had already used her ample weight to shove the other animals toward the front of the truck and away from the draft from the exposed rear. The cold, crisp morning air held the sweet aroma of steaming manure and sweat. Ice caked around the animals' mouths, crusting the green alfalfa slime along their lips. It was cold.

The November rutting season was on. The big old "mosshorns" in the high country would be a bit less wary. Like human males, big mule deer bucks tend to think with those two brains between their legs when chasing females during rut.

Mule deer are not stupid. That's a misconception. They have a tendency to move at all hours of the day during rut and are distracted enough to enable hunters to stumble across them more often. Their curiosity is more intense. No use passing up any potential doe.

We reached the 6,000-foot level in late morning after a steep ride from the truck. Deer tracks were few along the forest service trail we had ridden. I couldn't believe deer could live that high and in snow up to my waist. This time I figured Will was wrong.

We tied the puffing and steaming horses and mules to four beefy alpine firs at the end of a long switchback on the trail. Will and I left Dal to tend the animals while we began our hunt by heading downhill through thick timber and windfalls. Dal was seventy-two that winter and tough as saddle leather, but an old logging injury prevented him from plunging through the thigh-deep snow with us in search of a buck. He would hunt close by the animals, knowing that occasionally deer, elk, and moose have been drawn to the sounds and smells of stock animals. Some cross-eyed rutting buck just might take a liking to Tinkerbell.

John Roskelley on Tinkerbell after a successful Hawkins' mule deer hunt in northern Idaho, 1980. (Photo by Will Hawkins)

We were on a south slope in a heavy stand of alpine fir when we cut the first, and only, track.

"It's fresh," Will whispered. "By the size of it, I'd say he was the buck we're looking for."

The animal had a good stride and a deep track. He was headed straight downhill with a purpose, as if to say, There's does down there and they're mine. The track disappeared into thick timber.

"Let's follow him and see if we can't catch him in bed," Will said.

Right, I thought. For twenty years I had chased white-tailed and mule deer throughout Washington, followed a lot of tracks, and not once did I find an animal standing in them. It's not that I didn't believe deer made tracks. But they were always too smart or I was too noisy for me to catch them standing in them.

My dad always gave me sound hunter advice, such as "Look under trees, not in the open" and "Walk slowly. Do more standing and sitting." But how do you believe someone, even your dad, when they never get anything?

So I was skeptical.

Will must have been, too. I was dressed in a nylon rain suit and, in the deep snow, sounded like a horse trough full of Rice Krispies and milk. Will could have said something, but that wasn't his way. He must have figured it would just be more of a challenge for him to get me a deer. Besides, if John Roskelley wanted to wear nylon, why not?

Will spotted the deer in his bed under a clump of thick alpine fir. Before he could grab my shoulder and point, the deer jumped. He pogo-sticked ten feet straight up and twenty feet sideways. We didn't look like does, and he didn't get that old from waiting around.

I had a split second to identify, shoulder my 7mm magnum, find some hair in the scope, and fire. I could have sworn I was pointed at tree bark when I pulled the trigger.

The deer was gone. I dashed downhill through a clearing just in case he had completely lost his mind and stopped to look. No such luck. Will came alongside me.

"You hit him," Will whispered. "It was a solid *whumpf.*"

Heard the bullet hit? That was a new one on me. There was no way I hit that deer. Scared him maybe. But Will insisted and waded over to the clump of trees.

There lay the buck, a deer so old he would have died that winter. His rack was deformed and many of his teeth were missing. He had massive front shoulders and a little rear end. He reminded me of the Incredible Hulk.

I never questioned Will's hunting strategy again.

April 1986

Will was moved from Sacred Heart Medical Center in Spokane to an outpatient clinic in Coeur d'Alene, Idaho, to be closer to his family, yet still have the care and treatment he needed for the constant debilitating pain. Joan worked in the Sandpoint post office days and drove thirty miles to Coeur d'Alene to be with Will at night. There seemed to be a possibility Will would recover enough to go home. It never happened.

The September bear season opened. I forced myself to go, but my thoughts never left Will, bedridden in Coeur d'Alene.

"How'd you do?" Will asked that weekend.

"I got a nice boar," I replied, smiling. "A five-and-a-half-footer and typical of the bear up there—all black."

"Boooooy," he said. "Dead-eye Roskelley. You never miss."

When I did miss, Will had a ready-made reason. "Bad crosswind, eh?," or "Scope get knocked?"

I was hunting alone now in the rimrock country and deep forests Will had shown me. It just wasn't the same. I knew I wasn't spotting a lot of animals Will would have seen. I missed his praise, his knowledge. I missed his presence.

Dal missed him a lot more. He and Will had been inseparable since Will was a little boy. They had a mountain behind Sunnyside and above Pend Oreille Lake they called "Our Mountain." There wasn't a trail they hadn't traveled together.

Except for this one. Dal would have taken Will's place in that bed without a word if he could have. But for some reason, it was Will's trail, and his alone.

It was the fall Ol' Hereford was spotted that Will first complained to me about feeling his age. We were loaded with eighty pounds apiece of meat from an elk his son, Bill, had shot. I passed it off as perhaps a cold virus. Besides, I was feeling a bit weak hauling that meat, too.

We went after Ol' Hereford a month later. The deer were gathered in their wintering yard. Tracks were everywhere on the steep, timbered hillside. Winter had come early to the high country and the snow was deep and the temperatures low.

"It's got to be Ol' Hereford," Will whispered. "Only he could make a track this big."

I kneeled in the deep fresh snow. The track stood out among the dozens marking the deer yard. It was deeper and wider, almost the size of a small elk's.

I followed the track into thicker huckleberry brush and bear grass and found his scrape. He had worked the area over good, pawing twice the area of an ordinary mule deer buck.

Will gave me a low whistle and waved. I waded through the snow over to him.

"He's headed uphill," Will said. "Let's see what he's up to."

Will followed the track closely, watching the thick timber all around us. A big buck likes to backtrack over his trail and bed down above it, watching for other deer or danger.

Ol' Hereford's track was fresh. His pellets were still steaming and soft. Will broke trail through the knee-deep snow for a hundred yards, then I took a turn. The big deer had gone directly uphill, hugging the low branches of hemlock and alpine fir.

I hadn't seen Will this excited in years. This buck was his Mount Everest. Will knew that even to see Ol' Hereford, he would have to use every tactic he had learned in more than thirty years of hunting.

He kept saying he wanted me to shoot him. But I wouldn't have done so. And I don't really think Will would have either. Knowing there was always an Ol' Hereford in the woods to chase was what the sport of hunting was all about.

Ol' Hereford must have known we were on his trail. He left the herd area and headed straight for a 7,000-foot ridge. Most bucks circle around and stay in the area.

Exhausted from the deep snow and steep climb, Will and I followed, hoping to get close. We never did. We left Ol' Hereford's track as it descended into the next drainage. He was too smart, too wary. Just the kind of buck we wanted Ol' Hereford to be. We swore we would return.

December 1986

"Go ahead, Will," I whispered. "Let yourself go."

Will's eyes remained fixed on the faded green ceiling. A suction tube worked overtime to remove saliva from his open mouth. He inhaled in a gasp, then exhaled slowly, pushing the air out with an involuntary groan. A sign he was still alive.

"I'll be with you one of these days and we'll chase Ol' Hereford 'til we drop. Just you and me and Ol' Hereford."

I wanted to tell him to keep fighting, not to quit, but I couldn't. He had fought too long and too hard. He was a shred of his former self. He deserved the truth.

I was told by a physician that sixteen months was the average life expectancy for a person diagnosed with multiple myeloma. It had been eighteen.

It was time.

I felt Will squeeze my hand lightly. He understood.

We buried Will on an open hillside on his dad's farm on Sunnyside. The deer are thick there. "Our Mountain" is plainly visible above the deep blue of Pend Oreille Lake, and Chimney Rock isn't far away. And neither are we.

There's no doubt in my mind that the following poem, "How Did You Die," by Edmund Vance Cooke, was written with friends like Will Hawkins and Kim Momb in mind.

> *Did you tackle that trouble that came your way*
> *With a resolute heart and cheerful?*
> *Or hide your face from the light of day*
> *With a craven soul and fearful?*

Oh, a trouble's a ton, or a trouble's an ounce,
Or a trouble is what you make it.
And it isn't the fact that you're hurt that counts,
But only how did you take it?

You are beaten to earth? Well, well, what's that?
Come up with a smiling face.
It's nothing against you to fall down flat,
But to lie there—that's disgrace.
The harder you're thrown, why the higher you bounce;
Be proud of your blackened eye!
It isn't the fact that you're licked that counts;
It's how did you fight and why?

And though you be done to death, what then?
If you battled the best you could;
If you played your part in the world of men,
Why, the Critic will call it good.
Death comes with a crawl, or comes with a pounce,
And whether he's slow or spry,
It isn't the fact that you're dead that counts,
But only, how did you die?

SEO HAD TRIED TO COMMIT SUICIDE BY CHEWING OFF
HIS TONGUE. INGENIOUS, I SUPPOSE, FOR SOMEONE
WHO COULDN'T MOVE ANYTHING BUT HIS MOUTH AND
WANTED TO SPEED UP THE INEVITABLE.

THE WIDOWMAKER

"I never thought freeze-dried stroganoff could smell so good," Jim Wickwire said.

I scooped another steaming spoonful into his frozen plastic cup and replied, "Enjoy it. I figure we've got another two days of food left before we're out."

Wickwire, a veteran of seven trips to Denali since 1972, propped himself onto an elbow at the vestibule end of our dome tent, closed his eyes, and savored his first bite. He knew, from having eaten hundreds of such meals on countless expeditions, that it would be all downhill from there.

Wick, as he's known to his friends, and I had

worked our way twelve miles up the Kahiltna Glacier in the first week of May 1992, from the airstrip at 7,200 feet to our 14,300-foot camp on the West Buttress Route, in eight days. Denali can be pleasantly warm, almost inviting, down low on the Kahiltna at this time of year, but our experience had not been that nice. Our packs and sleds of gear had been heavy and the new snow difficult to walk on. A short, fierce four-day storm had pinned us down at our 10,000-foot camp, cut visibility to ten yards, dumped a foot of fresh snow, and dropped temperatures to minus ten degrees. I was quickly learning again, eleven years since my first trip to Denali, just how cold it could get near the Arctic Circle in early May.

Except for a four-hour hike down to our cache at the Northeast Fork and back to retrieve more food and a larger dome tent, we had hibernated in our small, two-man mini-dome during the storm. The few pounds we had eliminated by taking the smaller tent above the Northeast Fork proved to be a boondoggle, as we soon tired of bumping shoulders, misplacing personal gear, and cooking while lying on our bellies. As experienced as we were, we had forgotten that comfort in such circumstances is worth the few extra pounds.

On May 9, the day after the storm, Wick and I had moved to 12,500 feet under clear skies, then to our present camp at 14,300 feet the following morning. The weather had cleared and stabilized, yet continued to be gusty and below normal temperature. It looked as though we could acclimatize for several days at that altitude, move back down to the Northeast Fork of the Kahiltna, and, after a few days' rest, have a go at our main objective, the Cassin Ridge. But Denali's unpredictable arctic weather severed our well-laid plans within hours of our arrival at 14,300 feet.

We had just excavated a site for our soon-to-be-pitched tent and were building a solid snow wall from the ice blocks, when a helicopter circled the camp and landed. Two rescue rangers in red one-piece jumpsuits crouched, walked to the chopper, climbed in, and flew off. The chopper circled for several minutes, gaining altitude, before disappearing over the ridge.

Spotting another ranger nearby communicating with the chopper, I moseyed over. "What's all the fuss about?" I asked Matt Culberson, a volunteer rescue ranger, who, along with his wife, Julie, another volunteer, was stationed at the camp with park rescue ranger Ron Johnson.

"We've got a frostbitten climber at 17,000 feet," he replied. "We'll pick him up, evaluate him, and probably take him to Anchorage."

"Well, if there's anything we can do to help out while we're here, let us know." I gave him our names and returned to camp to help Wick set up the tent.

This was the second day of perfect weather, and up and down the mountain climbers were taking advantage of it to make headway. The four-day storm had created a bottleneck of climbers from the airstrip up to 11,000 feet. Now, to make up for lost time, we were all moving en masse toward 14,300 feet, a major acclimatization camp.

Upon our arrival, Wick and I had chosen an isolated spot away from the main camp to ensure us peace and quiet. But before we were settled in for the night, so many others had arrived and camped nearby that we were just another tent near the outskirts of a growing urban tent sprawl.

The camp teemed with activity. As I plopped down in the snow and took a breather from stacking ice blocks to protect our tent, a large group of Koreans, burdened under loads destined to be left at 17,000 feet, lined up next to our campsite, then began cramponing toward the well-trodden route. Within minutes of their departure, ropes of Germans in battalion strength arrived from below, staking out a territory near our camp big enough to require a zip code. Around us we could hear voices talking in French, Hindi, Swiss-German, and other languages. By nightfall, it was truly an international camp.

Fifteen hundred feet above us, climbers ferrying loads to upper camps lined up for their turn to use the only fixed ropes on the West Buttress Route. From my vantage point, they resembled small ants moving to and from their nest. Those heavily loaded and climbing upwards were slow and plodding, while climbers on their way back to camp descended effortlessly, almost falling from the ridge crest.

"Wait a minute, Wick," I said, watching two particularly fast descenders. "I think those two in the middle slid out of control. One of them looks hurt."

I was right. Before the first rescue was completed and the frostbitten climber brought to camp, word was received by the rangers that an American climber had slipped, fallen a short distance, and broken his arm. The chopper pilot unloaded his first passenger, then flew to the accident site above camp. He hovered at 15,000 feet, placing one of his skids on the slope, while the injured climber was loaded into the chopper. He was then flown back to the ranger camp for treatment and later evacuation to Anchorage along with the original frostbitten climber.

"I can see right now there's one big difference between here and the Himalaya," I said. "Rescue. You're on your own in the Himalaya. Here, you can be picked off the slope and be in Anchorage within the hour."

"That's the West Buttress Route for you," Wick replied. "But let me tell you, you're on your own on less traveled routes."

Wickwire was painfully aware of the rescue possibilities elsewhere on Denali. In May 1981, Wickwire and twenty-five-year-old Rainier guide Chris Kerrebrock had flown to Denali to attempt a new route on the seldom-climbed Wickersham Wall. After following the standard route up the Kahiltna Glacier to 10,000 feet along with hundreds of others climbing the West Buttress, they dropped over Kahiltna Pass onto the Peters Glacier, a seldom-visited area of Denali. While descending the Peters, tragedy struck.

"We were trying to make our way over to a lateral moraine through a heavily crevassed section of the glacier," Wick recalled. "The sled Kerrebrock was towing kept tipping over, so we had shortened the rope between us to about twenty-five feet so I could turn it back over. After slowly crossing a particularly bad crevasse field, we dropped off a slight rise in the glacier and quickened our pace on what looked like a clean, smooth slope. I was trying to keep the rope free of the sled when I suddenly realized that I was pitching downward. I instantly knew we were both falling into the same crevasse and had only one fleeting thought: 'This is it.' The next thing I can recall is slamming down on

Jim Wickwire at 16,000 feet on the West Buttress of Denali, 1992.

top of Chris and the sled twenty-five feet down in a shoulder-width crevasse."

Kerrebrock had walked into the narrow crevasse at a slight angle, fallen forward, and was now wedged like a cork by his shoulders and pack while facing down horizontally. As far as Kerrebrock knew, he was uninjured, but he complained to Wickwire that he couldn't feel his left arm. Wickwire could see that it was trapped between his pack and the wall of the crevasse.

Despite a broken left shoulder, which made his arm nearly useless, Wickwire managed to bend and contort within the narrow confines of the crevasse enough to remove the crampons from his pack and put them on his feet. With equal difficulty, he released his ice hammer from the sled.

"The crevasse was only eighteen inches wide and very cramped," he continued. "I couldn't just frontpoint out because there was no room to swing my feet, so I chipped small, half-inch-deep pockets for my frontpoints all the way to the top. I was afraid I would fall back on top of Chris, but I took my time and it paid off."

Once on top, Wickwire set up a haul system with jumars and a picket, hauled his pack to the surface, then tried to move Kerrebrock. He wouldn't budge.

"I went back down into the crevasse on jumars to see if I could free Chris by manipulating his pack or by using my body weight and the strength in my legs. Nothing I did or could do moved him in the slightest."

They had fallen into the crevasse at close to 3:00 P.M. Although greatly agitated by his predicament, Kerrebrock stayed calm throughout the ordeal, even when he realized he was not going to get out alive.

"After several hours of futile effort, we both realized Chris was going to die. He talked about his family and how much he loved them. This was the most painful experience of my life. In not freeing Chris from his icy trap, I felt an overwhelming guilt and sense of failure," Wickwire recalls.

"At one point, Chris made me promise not to leave the crevasse because if I was to fall into another one and disappear his family would never know what happened to him. He died sometime after midnight from hypothermia."

Wickwire stayed next to Kerrebrock for five days with only a partially filled bottle of water, a bit of jerky, some jam in roll-up tubes, and pilot bread. It was all he could retrieve from the sled below with his injured shoulder.

"On the fifth day," Wickwire continued, "I left a note describing the accident attached to the picket and began retracing our steps up the Peters Glacier. I had to try to get out because my attempts to contact overhead planes by radio had not worked. Within a couple of hundred yards, I partially fell through another crevasse. Kerrebrock's concern had almost proved to be true. From that point on, I probed every foot of snow while on my hands and knees, then returned for my pack a short distance behind me."

A major ice avalanche off the mammoth wall above him nearly engulfed him. Later, while traversing the middle of the Peters, a severe arctic storm pinned him down for five more days. For the second time in his life, the bivouac sack that had saved his bacon on K2 in 1978 came to his rescue.

Two weeks after their plunge into the crevasse, Wickwire, malnourished and exhausted, was able to make radio contact with Doug Geeting, who was flying over to the Wickersham to check on their progress. Geeting thought he was calling from the summit.

"When Doug found out what had happened to Chris, and finally spotted my position, he dropped that plane onto the Peters without hesitation and taxied right over to where I stood. It was only then that I knew I had made it."

Wickwire knew rescue was a longshot on the Peters. Like climbers in the Himalaya or other remote areas, he and Kerrebrock were dependent on each other and weren't relying on the park service or other teams of climbers. But the attitude among those climbing the West Buttress seemed to be different. Why? Perhaps because most climbers on the West Buttress are relative novices to high altitude and severe weather. Maybe it's because there's ranger assistance at 14,300 feet and a helicopter available to anyone in trouble. Who knows? I do know that too many climbers, novices and experts alike, climb unroped up the glaciers; too many ignore the signs of bad weather; and too many treat Denali like an oversized Mount Rainier. Denali is a dangerous mountain.

In two days the camp had grown into a small tent city, with close to a hundred climbers of ten different nationalities. I hadn't seen this kind of activity since 1974, when 180 climbers from eleven nations gathered for a month of climbing in the Russian Pamirs.

There were so many parties in snow caves, tents hidden behind massive snow walls, and the camp was so spread out on the flat glacier, that the only sure way to determine the quantity of climbers in camp was by how long the line for the only privy was during peak morning hours. In as exposed a place as the 14,300-foot camp, there was no way to avoid sitting three feet above the snowfield on the park service's plywood throne and relieving yourself, while half the camp milled nearby in the cold waiting their turn. By the time the storm arrived, the line was endless.

The same evening we arrived in camp, Wick returned from the ranger hut with good and bad news. "The bad news is that the rangers have received word that the worst storm in a hundred years is expected to hit the mountain tonight or early tomorrow morning and last for a week."

"Great, just great," I replied. "What the hell are we going to do for food? We don't have enough to last out a long storm and still get to the summit."

"Well, the good news is we've been invited for ham dinner tonight," Wick said. "And after mentioning to Johnson that the storm would put us short on food, he promised to help us out if worst came to worst."

The storm blew in that evening, plummeting temperatures to forty and fifty below within hours. To make matters worse, the cyclone-strength winds that had gained momentum over the arctic waters of the Bering Sea hit Denali at more than one hundred miles per hour, manhandling tents not protected by snowblock walls, burying others under dunes of spindrift, and making camp life more difficult than it already was. The wind chill factor disappeared off the chart and was estimated at minus 150 degrees Fahrenheit and lower.

During brief lulls throughout the nine-day storm, impatient climbers with tent fever set off up the route to acclimatize or carry a load to the next camp. As antsy as I get by sitting, I knew better than to expose myself to potential frostbite and hypothermia in the continuing subzero temperatures and wind. But I wasn't surprised by the others' actions, as there were many inexperienced climbers in camp who had taken Denali too lightly.

I emerged from our tent each morning fully dressed to dig us out of our nightly snowdrift, get a breath of fresh air, and reenergize after hours in the horizontal storm position. Many throughout camp would do the same, except that rather than prudently taking cover after a short time and returning to their tent to stay warm, they hung about outside for hours talking, putzing, and getting colder, as if this was a test of their will to summit Denali. I figured it was a simple test of their experience in the mountains.

"Maybe in our old age, Wick, we've just turned into wimps."

"No, Roskelley," he replied, "we just know better after all these years."

Wick had just taken that first bite of stroganoff on May 17, seven days into the storm, when I heard the quarrelsome squawk of boots biting hard, cold snow quickly approaching the tent. The sound stopped at our tent door.

"Hey, Jim, John," Johnson said. "We just got a report that several Koreans have fallen in a crevasse. Do you want to go up and help?"

Wick and I looked at each other, then at the stroganoff steaming on our plate. I shrugged my shoulders, giving Wick the okay to speak for me too. "You bet," Wick replied. "When do you want us?"

"Matt and Julie, along with a couple of Koreans, are heading up now. If you could join them as soon as possible, I'd appreciate it. I'll be staying here in camp in case you need more gear or manpower at the scene later on."

As Johnson left, Wick and I put down our unfinished dinners, pulled on our boots, dressed from head to toe in everything we had, and crawled from the warmth of our tent into the bone-chilling minus-fifteen-degree temperature, gusting winds, and whiteout of the storm. It was six o'clock by the time Johnson had given us a radio, additional rescue gear, and we were roped up and on our way. The other rescuers were long gone somewhere up the slope and into the storm.

Followed closely by two more Koreans, Wick and I blindly negotiated the flat snowfield out of camp by memory, found a trail wand near the beginning of the slope, and climbed upward. A sudden, brief clearing in the thick cloud revealed the other rescue team far off route to our left. A radio call brought them in our direction and, within minutes, we were together cramponing steeply upward in an effort to find the missing climbers.

Julie reached the crevasse first. "I see one of them," she yelled to us. "He's trapped at the waist about eighty feet away. You won't believe this hole."

It took several minutes longer for Wick and me, not quite as acclimatized as the Culbersons, to reach the lip of the crevasse. The scene below would have made a great opening to an Alfred Hitchcock thriller. Not only was it frightening for the Koreans who were trapped within the crevasse, but I knew that it was going to be dangerous for us as well. I couldn't help thinking that I should have finished my stroganoff, gone to bed, and let the rangers do their duty. But it was too late. The one Korean was still alive and in need of help.

What Wick and I, and hundreds of other climbers on the mountain for the past several weeks, had thought was a solid shelf of snow over a small ten-foot crevasse, proved to be a gaping wound in the glacier 150 feet in length, 40 feet wide, and 60 feet deep. No telling how much deeper it actually was because the snow and ice bridge had fallen in and plugged the crevasse, trapping the two Koreans. Why they weren't buried under the hundreds of tons of ice blocks around them remains a mystery to all of the rescuers.

The Koreans were guilty of one thing—being in the wrong place at the wrong time. They had stopped on the only flat spot along the wanded route to the ridge, and, after weeks of mountain climbers walking and stopping to eat or rest on it, the bridge had suddenly collapsed under their weight. But it wasn't just their weight. After seven days of storm, the low-angled snow bridge hiding the crevasse had accumulated tons of drifting snow and slough from the steep slope above. The Koreans were just the proverbial straw.

During a lull in the storm, Wick and I, in an effort to get some exercise, had climbed to the same spot and stopped just short of the now collapsed area for lunch along with ten others who stopped right over its middle. I had noticed that the flat area was in line with small crevasses exposed on each side of the glacier, so I sat on my pack on solid ice near the slope we had just come up. The area was innocent-looking enough, but it bothered me anyway. Few other climbers paid any attention to the possible danger and many were crossing it unroped.

I asked Wick to lower me into the crevasse so I could try throwing the one Korean a rope. After all, he was only trapped to his waist, and perhaps we could avoid risking our necks by descending into the crevasse. It didn't work. I couldn't throw it that far accurately and the Korean was obviously cemented in by the weight of the ice. A team of draft horses wouldn't be able to pull him out of his predicament.

Matt rappeled to the bottom, tested the false floor, then unhooked from his line and hustled over to the trapped man. I did the same a few minutes later, preferring to stay tied-in to my safety line just in case the floor shook loose and dropped another hundred feet with me in it.

Seong Yu Kang, the Korean, had dug a conical pit around his waist with a Swiss Army knife, but was a long way from extricating himself. It had already been three hours since the accident and, even though there was little wind deep in the crevasse, the air temperature was minus fifteen degrees and hypothermia was quickly setting in.

Matt, hearing moaning from beneath ice blocks under the overhanging upper wall twenty feet away, went searching for the other climber, while I, along with Kang's help, dug madly around him with our only shovel. With the ice block floor settling as we moved about, and the eighty-foot-high upper wall overhanging us the width of the crevasse, it was not hard to work faster than normal, despite being at 15,000 feet. I wanted out of that hole.

"The other one's alive," Matt yelled to me, "but he may not make it. He looks pretty bad."

As Matt lifted what ice blocks he could off Dong Choon Seo and tried to determine the extent of his injuries, I finished digging Kang out. I had to give Kang credit. He wanted to stay in the crevasse to help dig out his buddy, Seo, in spite of having been trapped in that awesome hole close to death for hours. Julie and Wick, more or less helped by the Koreans with them, pulled him out with a three-to-one pulley system that they had set up on the glacier above.

As soon as Kang was anchored and on his way out of the crevasse, I scrambled over the ice blocks to Matt and Seo. Seo was trapped within a body-formed ice cave with a three-hundred-pound block of ice along his right side and pinched by lesser-sized blocks around him. Matt, using only his hands, had worked for twenty minutes to free Seo's face and left arm from the ice.

It wasn't easy to be near the Korean. Seo was moaning and crying loudly anytime he wasn't letting out banzai-like screams. He must have figured we were going to leave him to die at any moment, because once his arm and frozen hand were free, he would try to grab Matt or me by the leg or arm at every opportunity.

Seo's mouth had bled profusely and the snow around his face was blotched and reddish brown. Along with the bleeding from his mouth, I thought he might have internal injuries, a possible broken pelvis, and, judging by the bend of his one visible leg, numerous broken bones. Not until later, when he was examined at the hospital in Anchorage, did we find out why he was bleeding from the mouth. Seo had tried to commit suicide by chewing off his tongue. Ingenious, I suppose, for someone who couldn't move anything but his mouth and wanted to speed up the inevitable.

"This is going to take some work. Let's get his buddies down here to help dig," I suggested to Matt.

"Can't," he replied. "Park policy. We have to do the rescue. Do you want to dig for a spell?"

Dig, hell. I wanted out of that crevasse, not deeper into it. I kept thinking I should have had some sympathy for Seo, but I came up totally blank. Maybe it was because Matt and I figured Seo would die before we could get him out. With possible injuries to his back and pelvis, hypothermia, and frostbite to his exposed hand and buried legs, I couldn't get excited about pulling him out to die in my arms.

So why was I risking my neck for this guy? Matt was doing so because it was his job. That's what he'd signed up for. But me? Maybe, just maybe, deep down inside me, I knew this guy had a family that loved him. It could be my son stuck like this someday and in need of help. I'd want whoever it was to give him every possible chance, no matter what his injuries. I had to believe that to stay in there and keep digging.

Matt tried to calm a panicky Seo by talking to him and holding his hand. This kept him from grabbing me as I worked to uncover his torso and legs. Each small chip or block of ice that I removed from the pit revealed another piece to the puzzle. As his boot became visible, I realized that the leg I was uncovering was his right leg, which changed the picture completely. His other leg wasn't caught under the three-hundred-pound block of ice, but underneath the ice beside me and easily freed. I dug to the left and found his other leg, which turned out to be as good as new.

Matt and I traded digging several times before I stepped into the hole, grabbed Seo's jacket at the sternum, then pulled and wrenched him from his icy hole.

"We'd better be careful with him," Matt said. "He may have a back injury."

"I'm trying to, but if we don't get him out soon, he's going to die on us," I replied. "Grab the other side of his jacket and let's drag him over to the ropes."

Time had passed quickly for us inside the crevasse. While we had been digging for Seo, Ron Johnson, along with Denali guide Brian Okonek, arrived at the lip of the crevasse with a Sked Sled, a heavy plastic roll-up rescue sled, and more gear. Seo would have to be hoisted out of the crevasse in the sled.

As Matt and I waited for the Sked and a sleeping bag to be lowered to us, we inspected Seo for injuries. Surprisingly, he was in good shape.

His legs weren't twisted awkwardly anymore and pressure on his pelvic bones didn't produce pain. But he was like a popsicle. Matt lightly lay on top of him to provide extra body warmth, while I found a hat and glove for his exposed flesh.

Seo was pulled out of the crevasse within minutes after we had zipped him into a sleeping bag and strapped him onto the sled. We kept him packaged and tied in the sled and slid him down fifteen hundred feet to camp within an hour and just before dark. Kang, helped down by three of his teammates, was already there enjoying packaged squid and other Korean delicacies.

Seo was given an intravenous saline solution by a doctor in camp, then transported to Anchorage the next morning by helicopter. We later found out by radio from the rangers in Talkeetna that Seo, although seriously hypothermic, had escaped with only a compressed vertebra, bumps, bruises, and minor frostbite.

During those first three weeks in May, the severity and length of the storm had created a series of problems for the rescue personnel and park service. On May 13, four days before our rescue of Seo and Kang and three days into the storm, a Korean party attempting a new route on the South Face found the body of Italian climber Roberto Piombo, who had apparently been blown off the Cassin Ridge. The body of his partner, Giovanni Calcagno, was spotted hanging in a tangle of ropes on May 16, during a helicopter rescue attempt to reach three Koreans stranded at 17,700 feet on the Cassin Ridge. Hurricane winds prevented the Lama from flying above 16,000 feet and the rescue was postponed until the weather stabilized.

Distress calls from the Koreans continued throughout the storm. Finally, on May 18, the Lama, at the top of its altitude limit, plucked the three badly frostbitten men off the ridge one at a time and landed them at 14,300 feet. They were then taken en masse by a Chinook helicopter to Anchorage. The rescue cost well over $100,000, and involved the use of five aircraft, including several reconnaissance planes, and scores of federal personnel.

The Koreans' experience on the Cassin Ridge parallels my own back in 1981, except that their philosophy concerning rescue and mine are miles apart. When Jeff Duenwald and I, both longtime Himalayan veterans, started up the Cassin Ridge, we didn't give a single thought to the possibility of being rescued by anyone other than ourselves.

Three days into our climb of the ridge and a day short of the summit, we were hit by one of Denali's vicious storms. Pinned down on a narrow, icy ledge below the exit gullies at 17,700 feet, in minus-forty-degree temperatures and hurricane winds, Jeff and I kept our tent in one piece for five days. Halfway through the storm, I began to go completely blind for periods of one minute every other minute. It was cerebral edema.

We didn't panic. Despite having only one 9mm rope, six rock pins, no food, and with me blind as a bat, we were determined to rappel the route. When the storm ended, Jeff and I packed our gear and headed down.

I rappeled first, taking the hardware to set up the anchors. Patience was important because I would have to sit tight hanging from the rope each time my eyesight left me, then quickly continue rappeling or placing hardware when it returned. After we had descended 3,000 feet in two days, my eyesight returned to normal. We reached the base of the ridge the next day, successfully completing our own rescue. My philosophy is simple: if you put yourself in jeopardy, then it's up to you to get yourself out.

The storm blew itself out on the evening of May 18, but Wick and I were too exhausted from the rescue to move up. Instead, we relaxed at 14,300 feet, shaved additional weight from already finely tuned loads, and searched the camp's vacated tent sites for scraps of food left by those who were retreating and didn't want to carry it down. By nightfall, we had one or two days' worth of discards and a good two days more of palatable goods from the rangers.

On May 19, we climbed steadily to 16,000 feet in a line of humanity that disgorged from 14,300 feet and ended abruptly, out of sight over the ridge. For some reason unknown to us, the climbers before us who had reached the ridge began to retreat back to camp. As we gained the ridge, we soon knew the problem. What had been a pleasant, sunny, windless afternoon on the lee slope above camp turned to hell on the windward side. A steady wind with sixty- to eighty-mile-per-hour gusts hit us, taking us to our knees. Everyone on the ridge was putting on their coats, strapping down their gear, and trying to stand up safely. It was impossible.

Wick and I couldn't retreat now. We had a limited supply of food and there was none left at the lower camp. The wind had to quit sometime, and when it did, we wanted to be in position to go for the summit. While others dumped their loads of gear and descended, Wick and I found a small, easy-angled slope and started cutting and hacking a tent platform. It had to be bombproof, with a solid ice wall to break the terrible wind.

Halfway through our building project, Brian Okonek, the Denali guide who had helped us rescue the Koreans, dropped to our platform from his ice cave above and offered us the tent platform next to his cave. One look at its six-foot walls and foot-thick ice blocks and we accepted. He moved his party into the cozy, secure cave, as Wick and I, along with four Brits, anchored our two tents to the ice with anything long and pointed and prepared to wait out the never-ending winds. We were pounded and beaten on by the wind for another three days.

"The wind is still strong," I yelled back to Wick from the open slope above camp on May 21, "but it's reasonable. Let's go."

Wick and I packed our remaining trail food, donned extra clothing, and began our 4,000-foot, seven-hour climb to the top. The ascent was pleasantly uneventful. The wind died completely as we reached the summit plateau, and with that good fortune our few minutes on top of North America's highest point were crowned in splendor by the endless ridges and glaciated valleys at our feet and, of course, only blue sky above.

We retreated back to our camp at 16,000 feet for one more night, then descended to our cache at 14,300 feet. The camp had not changed its vagrant character, only its occupants. Sadly, Johnson informed us that Mugs Stump, one of America's top alpinists, had been killed on the South Buttress in an accident all too reminiscent of the way Kang and Seo had been trapped—collapsing ice in a crevasse. To make matters worse, the Culbersons, on their descent after climbing the West Rib to break away from rescue duties for a few days, had found three dead Koreans in a crevasse on the Orient Express Route. The Koreans had fallen thousands of feet by the looks of their injuries.

All in all, eleven climbers died on Denali during the 1992 season, setting a single-season record. Seven were killed in the three weeks Wickwire and I were on the mountain, waiting out storms for our chance to summit. Weather obviously contributed to the accidents, but, in my opinion, poor judgment and inexperience played definite roles in all but two of the deaths.

We quickly packed up the gear we had left at the 14,300-foot camp that afternoon and made a dash for the airstrip, passing hundreds of climbers on their way up the glacier. We were tired of the cold, the wind, the hunger, climbers' errors, and death. As we departed, the *whumph, whumph, whumph* of the rescue chopper, pulling bodies from the Orient Express, sent us down the glacier with a chilling serenade. Denali, that great con artist, was now warm and quiet, bathed in sunshine, waiting to have more fun and games with the next batch of unsuspecting climbers. Human nature being what it is, they were on their way.

I WASN'T DEAD. I WASN'T EVEN INJURED. BUT MY
HEART, BEATING AT THE SPEED OF A HUMMINGBIRD'S
WINGS, STILL WANTED OUT. IT DIDN'T WANT TO
LIVE INSIDE AN IDIOT ANYMORE.

THE ART OF RISK

Mountain climbing rates a flat five on my risk scale of one to ten. Among recreational activities, I consider it a tad more risky than a day of skiing, but no match for an injury-prone pickup game of basketball with a bunch of aging jocks. But then, risk is relative to experience, conditioning, and, of course, who you're with.

I can significantly reduce the chance of an accident by climbing with someone who would rather not be a cover model for the American Alpine Club's *Accidents in North American Mountaineering*. Whoever said that a person can be his own worst enemy was never tied to a rope with some of the Wile E. Coyote types that I have met in twenty-eight years of mountaineering. I've been stuck with enough of them on many expeditions. Among other criteria, I now use the Roskelley "shoelace test." If a prospective partner's shoelaces don't stay tied, I don't tie into a rope with him.

There are other factors that I take into consideration each time I enter the mountains, such as route selection, weather, objective danger, fatigue, and equipment, to mention a few. But as far as I'm concerned, my choice of a climbing partner is by far the most important in reducing risk.

I'm frequently asked by the news media, "Have you ever been close to death?"

"Sure," I reply. "Every time I mingle with the general public on a freeway."

Disappointment follows. Reporters, like piranhas, are looking for blood-and-guts stories of people trapped at the bottom of crevasses, buried under tons of ice, or made into hamburger on a rock ledge by a car-sized boulder. These things happen.

Truth is, I know too many climbers who have been killed by those and other means, which has a tendency to awaken me to those dangers even more than I already am. I also have gotten into the habit of writing in my address book the names and addresses of climbers at the top of the sport in pencil. It saves having to replace the book every few years.

Personally, I've had very few close calls in the mountains. I like to think this can mostly, but not entirely, be attributed to my taste in climbing partners. I also reduce my risk by choosing technically difficult routes that are free of avalanche danger, icefalls, and crevasses, rather than easier, usually more objectively dangerous routes. Along with those two factors, a great deal of experience and one hell of a lot of luck help.

Twice I've had one foot on the other side of the chopping block and neither incident involved mountaineering. In both cases, it was my carelessness and inexperience that almost ended my life.

My first close encounter was when I was fourteen. I bought a Honda 50cc trail bike. It cost me everything I had earned for two years on my morning paper route, but it was worth every nickel. When my dad gave me the okay, that money departed from my pocket like a spooked trophy white-tailed buck during hunting season.

My dad's rule was "No driving on the streets until you get your license." That was fine by me. He was the outdoor editor for a local paper, so on weekends I accompanied him to various fishing hot spots throughout the Northwest. The trail bike kept me entertained while he wore out the palm of his hand tossing a fly over the water. I had to be moving, sticking my nose into every cave, turning over every rock.

It was well over one hundred degrees Fahrenheit early on a September morning in 1963 when my dad and I arrived at the mouth of the Grande Ronde River, thirty miles up the Snake River from Lewiston, Idaho. The Bastille-like, rust-colored basalt cliffs rose in tiers thousands of feet above the banks of the rivers, trapping the dry, stifling heat.

It's Hells Canyon country. Thorn bushes, cacti, rattlesnakes, and black widow spiders inhabit a land only the Nez Perce Indians considered home. But within this habitat years ago was some of the best mule deer, chukar, and quail hunting in the Northwest, not to mention unsurpassed steelhead fishing.

I had hunted chukars along the "breaks" of the Snake and the Grande Ronde for years. Chasing them up the nearly vertical canyons was perhaps part of the reason for my excellent lung power. Chukars inhabit terrain resembling the upper pitches of the Grand Teton. I'm sure I must have climbed my first unroped fifth-class pitch while hefting an eight-pound Browning 12-gauge automatic in pursuit of a covey of uphill-sprinting chukars. Then, just as I would be three-pointed on nearly vertical basalt, they would jump and sail down canyon like a flight of F-16s. Bird-dogging chukars on a hot September day is the toughest sport I know.

Dad helped me unload the Honda from the trunk, then grabbed his fly rod and disappeared down the bank of the river wearing a pair of those olive-drab pants all fathers seem to disgrace their kids with. You know, the baggy, worn-to-a-shine trousers John Steinbeck's characters wore in the movie *The Grapes of Wrath*. It would only be a few minutes before he reached his favorite "hole," called the "Pig's Sty," where he would toss his homemade barbless-hooked fly into the river hoping to entice a monster steelhead. I turned the key on the Honda, kicked the starter, and turned upstream along the Grande Ronde River.

The gravel country road was as barren as a moraine and devoid of life. Even the insects had had enough sense to take shelter from the sweltering canyon heat. It was a dead-end road used most frequently by local farm vehicles and an occasional fisherman or hunter during season. The roostertail of dust rose off the road like thick smoke, then hovered and spread outward, refusing to settle, as if it was enjoying the fresh air.

I pushed the little engine to its limit, reaching forty-five on the straightaways, skidding into the corners, and watching for mounds of loose pea gravel that could throw me faster than a sore-footed rodeo bronc. It was on my way back after several hours of cruising that I made my nearly fatal error.

I had crossed a short bridge that straddled a side creek on my way up the canyon. It was a ninety-degree approach onto the bridge and another sharp corner continuing up the river. On the return trip I forgot about the bridge. I was red-lining the throttle around a small bend shaded with a thicket of thorny trees when I found myself just a "What? Oh, shit!" short of the bridge.

I didn't panic. It takes time to panic and there wasn't any. I briefly hoped to skid into the turn and pull it out on the planking of the bridge. But no such luck. The pea gravel might as well have been ice. I wasn't going to make that bridge.

I had two choices. Die this way or die that. It looked like it made no difference. Either I had to hit the beachball-sized rocks used as a guard rail approaching the bridge sideways or turn the wheel and take the rocks head on. I wasn't a good enough rider to lay the bike over on its side. Regardless, I was going to take an unknown and invisible plunge into the void.

I turned the wheel.

Sound ceased the instant my front wheel smacked the boulder. I became airborne. The motorbike and I arced up like a basketball heading for the hoop, then my rear slowly left the seat as momentum threw me forward. My hands remained glued to the handlebars and I refused to let go. Don't ask me why.

There was no water running in the creek twenty-five feet below. I tried to scream, but it was like my heart had already got the picture and was making a beeline out of my mouth. Not a squeak escaped.

I remember thinking this is going to hurt and, boy, is my dad going to be pissed. Then I rotated over the handlebars, let go, and smacked full out on my back—in a four-inch-deep mud puddle. It broke my fall.

Whatever air I took in sailing into space exploded from my mouth on impact. I might as well have been 20,000 leagues under the sea rather than sitting in four inches of water. I couldn't get any air. My brain finally said to the muscles surrounding my lungs, "Let go, let go!" and I sucked in the deepest breath of my life. As the air rushed in to fill empty lungs, sound burst into my head. While I was splashing and gasping for breath, the crashing of metal and plastic finally ceased behind me. I wasn't dead. I wasn't even injured. But my heart, beating at the speed of a hummingbird's wings, still wanted out. It didn't want to live inside an idiot anymore.

The Honda had taken a beating. The front wheel rim was imitating the letter "D," the handlebars were turned ninety degrees to the wheel, and my clutch lever was gone. Little red and black pieces of Honda decorated the river rock around me. Needless to say, it wouldn't start.

It took me the rest of the day to wheel the Honda back to the Pig's Sty and my dad, who could wait all day to catch a fish, but was fuming after having waited several hours for me to show up. I don't think he ever realized how close his only son came to becoming rattlesnake fodder in a deep canyon on the Grande Ronde River.

The second time I came close to getting killed (and I still feel queasy when I think of it) was in 1987. I was on a *Field & Stream* magazine shoot for its advertising supplement, "The Guide to Camping." I was the writer and one of the models for the piece.

The crew of three agency personnel, a photographer, and an editor had been working several days photographing scenes of Dan Ford—my brother-in-law—and me using various advertisers' products, such as clothes, tents, and canoes.

We were in remote Nahanni National Park, located in Canada's Northwest Territories. The park is accessible only by canoe, a long backpack, or floatplane, so the magazine had hired and retained for the week a de Havilland Twin Otter with water pontoons owned by Simpson Air Charter Service. It was a decadent but great way to see one of the world's most beautiful, yet restricted, national parks.

As a prelude to the major debacle, I warmed up with a small potential disaster. It's days like this one that make me wonder how I survived all these years.

The photographer requested a reasonably sized campfire for a camp shot on the river's edge. It had been raining in the Mackenzie Mountains for days and dry wood was nonexistent. Gasoline seemed the only solution. I poured some gasoline into a drinking cup and when the

De Havilland Twin Otter and crew in Nahanni National Park, Northwest Territories, 1987.

photographer, who was set up across the lake, yelled for me to flare the campfire and freeze for the photo, I threw it onto a small previously lit fire.

The explosion took both Dan and me by surprise. Gas had spilled onto my hand and trousers when I had thrown it onto the fire and I instantly found myself engulfed in flames. I fell back onto the beach and dowsed the fire in the lake, but not before receiving second-degree burns that later raised large blisters on my fingers and hand.

I was taking a brutal ribbing for that mistake as we flew east along the Nahanni River for our next shoot. No one takes as much shit as an "expert" who screws up. It's like Michael Jordan tripping on the foul line or Walter Payton being tackled behind the line of scrimmage. It's time for the armchair crowd to get even.

The pilot banked the gaudy yellow-and-black Twin Otter low over three-hundred-foot-high Virginia Falls, buzzed upriver to look for landing hazards in the water, then brought the plane in for a smooth landing. He taxied downriver toward a steep mud bank crowded with five canoes and ten paddlers. The Otter's nose swung into the current as the pilot skillfully maneuvered the left pontoon toward the bank. The canoeists scrambled up and down the mud bank pulling their canoes away from the plane and ducking as the wing sliced back and forth over the embankment. They were angry.

I felt a bit sheepish sitting in a two-million-dollar plane and pushing canoeists off the river, people who had paddled hundreds of miles to see a pristine and unspoiled land, but it was the only spot to anchor the plane. The pilot pulled in like a taxi driver grabbing the only parking spot on Park Avenue—without hesitation and without consideration for the canoeists. The copilot, a young guy not long out of pilot school, jumped out the back door to anchor the pontoon next to the bank. Dan was out a few seconds later to give him a hand. I was right behind. In the eyes of those canoeists we must have seemed the epitome of tourists.

There was an eerie silence as the pilot feathered or rotated the props forward and backed the plane along the bank and the copilot slammed in a large metal stake and tied it to the back of the pontoon. Then there was a roar as the plane pulled forward.

I have not been around many planes. I saw the copilot finish securing the back of the pontoon, then dash up to the top of the bank and around the wing. My instinct, as usual, was to help. As the copilot and Dan climbed the bank and skirted the wing, I realized they were going to pound in another metal stake and tie down the front pontoon.

I thought, "Why not walk forward and have them throw me the line?" I had the only rubber boots, so the depth of the water and mud, which is why I thought they had run around the wing, would not be a problem for me. I walked toward the front of the wing. The props again feathered in a neutral position to let the bank eddy slowly float the plane upstream and tighten the back anchor. With the props in the neutral position, not a sound or a breeze emanated from them, which would have triggered some concern. I was already used to the roar of the engine.

As I walked out from underneath the wing, a short, dreadful scream came from the bank above. There was absolute terror in that cry. The scream was instantly followed by another equally chilling yell of "Nooooo!"

I froze instantly.

My first thought was perhaps someone on the bank had been hit by the wing. But, no, everyone there was looking at me—in horror. Two inches from my face was the prop. A blur of transparent yellow and black. For the second time in my life I felt the closeness of death. A fraction of time—a movement forward—was all it would take.

I backed up slowly, glancing at the copilot, who had screamed and saved my life, and at my brother-in-law, who had yelled "No," thinking it was too late. He would have had to explain to my sister how her expert mountain climbing brother had cheated death all these years only to die taking a bite out of a prop, which promptly splattered his brains against the side of a plane. Equally horrified expressions stared at me from the plane's windows. The others had also assumed I was walking to my death.

That was too close a call. It was days before I stopped thinking of that moment before the prop. It scared me as has no other incident in my life. There was no reason for it to happen. Just carelessness and circumstance.

I've had my share of potential climbing disasters too, based on a number of factors. For one, nature has its ways of telling you it's in control. Just one baseball-sized rock sailing past my face reminds me who has the upper hand.

And then there's the human carelessness that we're all subject to. I remember quite well the time I watched my rope slither down the almost vertical slabs beneath the Washington Column in Yosemite Valley as I carried a duffel bag of gear over my shoulder up to the first bivouac. I had failed to double my bowline and it had come loose. Straddled between two small footholds on 5.7 terrain with one hand, I vowed never to tie into my swami belt with anything less than a figure eight from then on. I made it to the bivouac.

Or the time I was rappeling off the buttress on Nanda Devi in India with Jim States after a full day of extreme climbing in bad weather. I started to leave the rappel stance that hung over the North Face when Jim yelled for me to stop and take a picture of him. I began wrapping the rappel line around my leg so I could let go with my hands, only to find out I had hooked my rappel gear into the short tail of excess rope left after the lead. Another ten feet and I would have taken the big ride down the North Wall and reached base camp in record time. Blame fatigue.

I also rely a lot on instinct, a kind of sixth sense. If I'm getting little vibes that make me uneasy, then it's time to take a second look.

All the experience in the world can't help me if I don't pay attention to that voice inside. My conscious self may not pick up on a potential disaster, but my inner self can—and does.

For instance, on Thanksgiving weekend, 1977, I was taking my family south from Spokane to Dr. Jim Morrissey's ranch in Stockton, California, for turkey dinner and quail hunting. I had even gone so far as to install a new stereo in my 1973 Saab. Three hundred miles into the trip I stopped to fill up with gas in Biggs Junction on the Oregon–Washington border. It was late afternoon, perfect driving conditions.

I drove south out of Biggs on Highway 97, climbing out of the Columbia River Gorge. Less than five miles up the canyon I felt something was wrong. At the same time, I couldn't seem to force myself to step on the gas. I pulled over.

"Joyce, I'm getting a real funny feeling," I said. "I'm not sick or anything. It's just that something is wrong and I can't seem to continue up the road."

We talked it out and finally decided to return to Biggs, have something to eat, and try again. I had no trouble turning around and driving back to Biggs.

A half hour later we got back in the car and started up the canyon again. I felt fine and couldn't understand the previous problem. Joyce and Dawn, my daughter, joked about me going batty as I sped up.

Within a hundred yards of where I had stopped previously the feelings mysteriously returned. Something was going to happen up the road. I was being warned. I had no choice but to pull over and stop again. It was as if a hand was grabbing my foot and taking it off the accelerator.

You may think I could ignore this. I couldn't. Twice I was stopped cold. There was no obvious reason, but there I was alongside the road unable to drive forward.

I listened to myself for a time, blocking out all input from Joyce and Dawn, which—as you can imagine—was considerable.

"John, maybe you've been to altitude once too often?" Joyce said.

"Yeah, Dad," Dawn chimed in. "You're losing it."

I knew there was a reason for what was happening. But it wasn't in this world.

"We're going home," I said and then swung the car around and headed back toward Biggs. The moment I turned the car, the vibes stopped. I was normal again.

Let me tell you, it wasn't easy to live with those two women that weekend. We searched the newspapers throughout the weekend for a major car accident on our intended route, or some type of disaster that had occurred, but there was nothing we could find. What made me stop and wouldn't let me continue, I may never know, but what's important is I listened.

There's nothing wrong with using old-fashioned sound judgment either. Take, for instance, my first trip to Everest with the 1981 American Everest East Face Expedition.

The first American expedition to the last great unclimbed face on Everest was well organized by the leader, Dick Blum, in terms of equipment, protocol, and personnel. No one would have guessed that torrential post-monsoon rains and blankets of snow would load the steep slope with treacherous avalanche conditions far into the climbing season.

The East Face, Everest's catch basin for moisture, removed its daily evening dose of snow with the early-morning sun each day. Snowfields, hundreds of acres in size, swept the face, fueled by gravity and traveling on cushions of air. At the bottom of the face, hundred-mile-per-hour winds preceding the avalanches exploded into our camps, twisting tent poles into giant paper clips and creating Carl Lewis–like track stars out of slothlike mountaineers.

Nor would one guess that the team, some of America's climbing immortals and legendary prima donnas, would succumb to personal ambition, inexperienced judgments, emotional interference, and, in general, amateurish mistakes.

I was among a group of four chosen by the team to reconnoiter a route up the lower face. We were to move to the base of the wall the next morning. I assumed the rest of the team would ferry loads in support. I was wrong.

Early the next morning climbers scrambled out of camp on their own reconnaissance, neglecting the fundamental approach to a large expedition—support. The idea of spending three or four nights at a yet to be established advanced base camp without supplies of food and equipment challenged my sense of teamwork. I abdicated my position on the first group in favor of ferrying loads for them and my successor.

I joined the advance team several days later. The day I arrived at advanced base carrying sixty pounds of personal gear, the four-man team descended off the buttress centered on the immense East Face, discouraged as a pack of wolves having missed their kill. We discussed the route in depth. It was in terrible condition, covered with deep, unconsolidated snow. The advance team decided to a man to pack up and descend to base camp in favor of abandoning the route. The North Ridge route, given to us as an alternative by the Chinese, was discussed as the logical second choice. I packed up my sixty pounds the next morning and, along with the others, descended to base.

At a group meeting later that afternoon the four-man team that had abandoned the route the night before decided to "give it another try." I must have been in a coma earlier. Didn't they tell me the route was too dangerous? Didn't I just carry my gear back and forth to base camp? They must have thought the danger on the face had gone away during our walk to base. Persuasive speeches by Kurt Diemberger, one of the world's foremost mountaineers, but acting as an ABC cameraman on this trip, and Sir Edmund Hillary, our honorary leader, did have a bit to do with their change in perspective.

It was here I planted my big size twelve and a half boot. The route was dangerously out of condition, leadership on the mountain nonexistent, and several of the key climbers had shown fatally poor judgment in route finding. I briefly hoped for a North Ridge attempt by the dissenters, but this proved unrealistic because of the lack of equipment and food. Going home was my only choice. I didn't want to discourage the climbers who were staying.

I wasn't a popular figure in camp after my decision to leave, but I was determined not to lose my life trusting the poor judgment of those around me. Who knows what possessed them. The ABC film? Triumph on the last unclimbed face on Everest? It wasn't good mountaineering sense for sure.

So I walked away from the East Face buried by an avalanche of self-doubt, accompanied by Kim Momb, Bruce McCubbery, and David Braeshears (who later returned because of his job with ABC as a cam-

eraman). My resolve was tempered in frustration, my motivation subdued by the team's indecision. As important as Everest was to my future
as a world-class mountaineer, the risk did not justify the means.

I, too, wanted that face more than anything on earth. I was on a roll.
My percentage of summits to attempts in the Himalaya was unsurpassed
and I was hungry for another. Technically, I was at my best. Physically,
an animal. But it was not to be.

The team that stayed eventually reached 21,000 feet before deciding
the route was in poor condition. The climbers prudently left Everest
weeks later and proceeded to Shisha Pangma, another 8,000-meter peak,
where they failed again.

Here again, team selection played an important part in the safety of
the expedition. Many of the climbers were proven professionals, yet their
judgment and safety were suspect in my eyes. Despite my desires, I chose
not to take the risk.

At this time in my life, I can't think of one peak worth really putting
my rear on the line for. And that's why I'm no longer among the world's
climbing elite.

The top climbs (not another "tourist" trip up Everest with gangs of
Sherpas and more oxygen bottles than ropes, but "guts hanging out
there" climbs) are high-stakes, risky endeavors. The climbers knocking
off these technical and mental/physical "impossibles" are taking big risks.
Many will get killed, and very few will continue climbing without a severe
accident or close call. Seldom do I have the "eye of the tiger" anymore.
I just won't take the necessary risks that are demanded by some of the
climbs being put up today.

Not too many years ago I took the occasional unnecessary risk. I was
young and seeing life through a one-inch-diameter tube of steel pipe.
"There's the summit, that's the route, here's how I'm going to get there."

At times I displayed an amazingly narrow point of view. I locked
onto summits like Scotty locking onto Captain Kirk with the transporter
on the *Enterprise*. Yet, despite my unrelenting push toward the top, safety

was the one constant on my mind among an array of potentially deadly variables. My rope mates will attest to this.

I like to think I've broadened my perspective, opened my eyes, and expanded my vision. Now I take the climb apart from beginning to end, studying the route, the rock, and the ice, and I know my partners' strengths and weaknesses. I treat the project as a job and a profession, not just another weekend outing.

In recent years, I've found that mountaineering is no longer a priority. My family, making a living, and investing time in the future are now more important to me than struggling for weeks at a time on some peak in central Asia. But, like so many of my contemporaries, I'm a risk junkie. I've been dependent on mountaineering to feed my ego for so long that withdrawal is still painful, although I've found that if I don't go climbing for a month, it doesn't hurt quite as much inside me anymore.

Over the years, climbing served as an important outlet for my intensely competitive nature and allowed me to exercise a sense of freedom I absolutely had to have. Subsequently, I have filled these obligations to my human nature with personal relationships and other sports, and require only an occasional climb to fulfill that part of my ego that ruled me for so many years.

GLOSSARY

A0 to A5: a rating system for aid climbing, with A0 the easiest.

acute mountain sickness (AMS): a symptomatic illness that can occur when the body tries to adjust to higher altitude.

advanced base camp (ABC): the second camp on an expedition, usually placed below a mountain's difficulties.

aid: a climbing technique that relies on pitons, chocks, aid slings, and similar equipment to hold part or all of a climber's weight in order to overcome difficult portions of a route; also known as artificial climbing.

alpinist: a mountaineer with rock, ice, and alpine climbing skills.

anchor: a solidly placed point of protection such as a piton or climbing nut, or a natural object such as a tree or rock, used as a belay. An anchor should be "bombproof," i.e., strong enough to resist any possible force it may be subjected to by a falling climber. Multiple anchors at a belay are standard.

angle: a V-shaped, hammer-driven alloy piton used in cracks of various sizes, depending on their width and taper.

ascenders: *see* jumars

Balti: a person from the Karakoram region of Baltistan, located in northern Pakistan.

base camp: the first and major camp set up on an expedition below any climbing difficulties; often referred to as B.C.

belay: the technique employed by an anchored climber of using a rope to safeguard his or her partner(s) from the effect of a fall. The device or point that anchors the rope is known as a belay.

bergshrund: the crevasse formed between a moving glacier and an upper snowfall.

bivouac: an unplanned overnight stay, usually with a minimum of comfort; also referred to as a bivy.

bolt: refers to a short, metal expansion bolt with threads on the exposed end that is driven into a predrilled hole in the rock. A bolt hanger is then secured to the bolt with a nut. The system is used for aid climbing, protection, and anchors.

bong: a wide-angle piton (two inches or wider) made from aluminum or steel.

bouldering: practicing rock climbing on short, sometimes very difficult routes with or without a rope, depending on one's boldness.

bridging: a climbing technique that uses opposing pressure against two walls to surmount wide chimneys, corners, and rock flakes.

carabiner: an oval or D-shaped metal snap link, one side of which opens by means of a metal spring clip, used for belaying, connecting runners, rappeling, et cetera; the universal attachment mechanism of climbing.

cardiopulmonary resuscitation (CPR): a procedure that reestablishes blood circulation and the movement of air into and out of the lungs in a pulseless, nonbreathing patient.

chimney: a vertical fissure, usually in a rock, but sometimes in ice, that is wider than a crack but narrower than a gully. Generally a climber can get his or her entire body into a chimney.

chock: *see* nut

cleaning a pitch: removing all protection from a lead.

cornice: deposit of wind-drifted snow on the lee edge of a ridge or other exposed terrain feature.

couloir: a gully within a mountain face or between ridges on a mountain, created by the erosion process.

crampon: a steel framework, usually with twelve sharp spikes, that fits over the sole of a boot and is held in place by straps or a binding; for use on snow and ice.

crevasse: a crack or opening, of any width, length, or depth, in the surface of a glacier.

decimal rating system: the American rating system for determining the difficulty of technical free climbing. The decimal system begins in Class 5 with 5.0 and continues to 5.14, with levels 5.10 through 5.14 each subdivided further with ratings of *a* through *d.*

dehydration: the loss of natural body fluids.

depth hoar: a weak and unstable form of snow that loses all strength when crushed and becomes very soft when wet due to its large, cup-shaped ice crystals.

dulfersitz: a method of rappeling in which a climber creates friction by using only a rope around his or her body.

executioner block: a rock boulder or flake precariously perched above a climbing route that is a potential deadly missile.

fist jam: a free-climbing technique of jamming a balled fist into an appropriate-sized crack to hold one's weight while climbing.

fixed rope: a length of rope anchored to the mountain and left in place for ascending or descending a section of the climb more than once.

flake: a section of rock detached from a larger body.

free climb: ascending a rock feature using only hands, feet, other body parts, and body positioning.

frostbite: the freezing or partial freezing of some part of the body. Ice crystals form between the tissue cells and cut down the supply of oxygen to minor blood vessels, leading to the deterioration and infection of the tissue cells. Tissue damage is inevitable.

frostnumb: a minor cold injury that is completely reversible by rewarming.

Gaurishankar: a 23,405-foot peak in the Himalaya range, located thirty-five miles due west of Mount Everest. It was first climbed by a joint Nepalese–American team in 1979.

glacier: the permanent, slow-moving ice associated with high or arctic mountain regions.

grade: the overall length and difficulty of a climb. There are seven grade levels, from Grade I, a short, several-hour climb, to Grade VII, a multiday, extremely technical ascent requiring experience, commitment, and boldness beyond the norm.

Grand Tetons: a range of peaks forty miles long and twelve miles wide, running north and south, located on the border of northwest Wyoming and northeast Idaho. The range includes the Grand Teton, Mount Moran, and Symmetry Spire.

harness: a system of high-strength webbing and buckles that fastens around the waist and, in conjunction with leg loops, supports a

climber's weight evenly throughout the mid-torso while suspended
or in the event of a fall.

haul bag: a large duffel made of durable fabric used to transport gear up
vertical cliffs by rope and pulley.

high altitude cerebral edema (HACE): swelling of the brain, probably
caused by increased blood flow to the brain and swelling of the
brain cells from hypoxia (oxygen deficiency). The most effective
treatment is immediate descent to a lower altitude. Constant
administration of bottled oxygen is a secondary alternative.

high altitude pulmonary edema (HAPE): leakage of blood plasma into
the lungs, which renders the air sacs ineffective in exchanging
oxygen and carbon dioxide in the blood. The most effective
treatment is immediate descent to a lower altitude. Constant
administration of oxygen is a secondary alternative.

Himalaya mountains: a mountain range that includes the highest mountains on the earth's surface, lying between India to the south and
Tibet to the north. It stretches fifteen hundred miles, from the
Indus River in the west to the Brahmaputra River in the east, and
has a width of about one hundred miles. The Himalaya lie in the
countries of India, Tibet, Nepal, Pakistan, and Bhutan. The name
comes from the Sanskrit words *hima* (snow) and *alaya* (abode).

hypothermia: the cooling of the body's core temperature.

icefall: an area of crevasses and seracs (large ice blocks) created by a glacier
flowing over a steep decline.

ice mushroom: a mushroomlike ice formation with a small base and a
larger top, the result of double cornices along an exposed mountain
surface such as a ridge.

ice plug: an ice formation that blocks the exit of a gully.

ice screw: a threaded, hollow-core alloy tube with an eye that can be
connected to a carabiner; used to protect or anchor a climber on
hard ice. Also known as an ice pin.

jam crack: a fissure in the rock small enough to insert a finger in or large
enough for balled fists or boots.

jamming: primarily a rock climbing technique that involves placing one or
a combination of body parts into a crack, then expanding that part
or parts by an opposing, flexing, or twisting motion.

jumar: a camming device with a handle that, when attached to a fixed
rope, enables a climber to ascend a rope but prevents the climber

from sliding down. Jumars are normally used in pairs. The word is frequently used as a verb, "to jumar," meaning to ascend using jumars or any similar device such as a Gibbs or Clogg.

Karakoram mountains: A vast complex of high mountains in the trans-Himalaya chain, lying east of the Indus River and west of the Yarkank River from Tibet's Kunlun mountains. The range is about 250 miles long and has nineteen peaks over 25,000 feet, including K2, the world's second-highest mountain.

knifeblade: a very thin and short-bladed piton.

lead: the distance between two belays a climber has to travel, also known as a pitch. A lead can vary from a few feet to the full length of a rope.

mountaineer: an alpinist with training in the disciplines of travel, outdoor living, and climbing in the mountains.

Mount Everest: the world's highest mountain (29,028 feet), which straddles the Nepal–Tibet border. It is named after Sir George Everest, a former Surveyor General of India. Nepal officially recognizes the peak as Sagarmatha, meaning "The One Whose Forehead Reaches up to the Sky," or, in Sanskrit, "Churning of the Ocean." China's official name for the mountain is Chomolangma, a word of Tibetan origin meaning "Lady of the Wind" or "Goddess of the Place."

Mount Index: a three-summited, 5,979-foot rock peak located on the western slope of the Cascade range in the state of Washington. The North Peak of Mount Index is known for its unusual brush holds and varied route problems.

Mount Moran: a 12,605-foot peak located in the northern portion of the Grand Teton range.

Mount Rainier: a 14,410-foot volcanic peak located in the Cascade range; the highest peak in the state of Washington.

Mount Robson: the highest peak in the Canadian Rockies, with an elevation of 12,972 feet. It is one of the most difficult peaks to summit by any route, and is considered one of the great peaks of the world.

Mount Shuksan: a 9,125-foot glaciated peak, composed of green schists and metamorphosed volcanics, located in the northern Cascade range of Washington State.

nail: to hammer in pitons.

Nanda Devi: a 25,645-foot Himalayan peak located in the Garhwal region of northwest India.

Nepal: a small, independent kingdom (54,362 square miles) located between India to the south and Tibet to the north, with a population of more than fifteen million people.

nuts: pieces of metal of various shapes and sizes attached to loops of rope, webbing, or cable, then attached to a climber's rope with a carabiner and used as protection when wedged into cracks. Also known as chocks.

off-width: a crack or fissure in a rock that no part of the body fits into securely while free-climbing.

open book: two rock faces joined by one corner and opening away from each other, usually at an angle of ninety degrees or more.

perlon: the tightly woven nylon outer sheath of a core-and-sheath climbing rope.

picket: a two- to three-foot length of extruded aluminum T-bar used as an anchor or for protection in hard snow.

pin: a piton.

Piolet USA: an ice-climbing tool developed by Yvon Chouinard and at one time sold by Chouinard Equipment.

pitch: *see* lead

piton: a tapered metal spike, available in a variety of sizes and shapes, that can be hammered into cracks in rock or directly into ice.

putz: to be in continual motion or disarray for no apparent reason.

rappel: to descend using a rope.

rime ice: a deposit of ice formed when droplets of water from the air freeze on rock.

rockfall: falling rock debris cut loose by erosion, wildlife, or climbers.

roof: an overhanging section of rock that is nearly horizontal.

rope: a rope specifically designed to hold the weight of a falling climber, usually 45 meters to 50 meters in length and either 9 millimeters, 10.5 millimeters, or 11 millimeters in diameter, with tensile strength varying from 3,500 pounds to 7,000 pounds.

sahib: a Nepali word that loosely means "sir."

serac: a block of loose ice broken away from the main portion of a glacier within an ice fall zone.

Sherpa: a race of people of Tibetan origin originally from Kham in eastern Tibet. They are Mahayana Buddhists, speak a Tibetan dialect, and have no written language.

solo climbing: climbing without a partner.

spindrift: fine, wind-blown snow.

talus: scree or loose rock accumulation on a slope.

Terrordactyl : a short ice hammer with a fifty-five-degree angle pick and a hammer head, developed in Scotland for severe to vertical ice climbs in frozen gullies.

tie off: to loop a short piece of webbing around a piton or other point of protection in order to reduce the fulcrum effect of a pull. The piton is then said to be tied off.

wands: lengths of small-diameter bamboo placed on glaciers or snowfields to mark a route.

windchill: the effect of a still-air temperature on exposed skin equalled by a combination of temperature and wind velocity. The harder the wind blows, the lower the temperature feels and the greater the rate of heat loss.

Yosemite Valley : a glaciated valley located in Yosemite National Park, in the state of California; a major tourist attraction because of the spectacular vistas of El Capitan, Half Dome, Yosemite Falls, and other features from the floor of the valley. Known among climbers as "the Valley."

Chronology of Major Events and Climbs

1965: Spokane Mountaineers Basic Mountain School

1966: Mount Thor, Gold Range, British Columbia, first ascent

1967: Chimney Rock, Selkirk Range, Idaho, first free ascent of East Face

1970: Dihedral Wall, El Capitan, Yosemite Valley

1970: Mount Dag, Valhallas, British Columbia, first ascent of South Face

1970: Mount Edith Cavell, Alberta, North Face

1970: Snowpatch Spire, Bugaboos, British Columbia, third ascent of South Face

1971: Liberty Bell, Independence Route

1971: Mount Howse, Alberta, second ascent of North Face

1971: Mount Chephron, Alberta, East Face

1971: North American Wall, El Capitan, 2.5-day ascent

1971: Graduated from Washington State University, Bachelor of Science, Geology

1972: Married the only woman who could possibly put up with me for the next twenty-seven years, Joyce Bakes, and became an instant father to her five-year-old daughter, Dawn

1973: Summited Mount Dhaulagiri (26,800 feet), Nepal Himalaya, world's seventh highest, third ascent

1974: Summited Peak Of The Nineteenth Party Congress (19,300 feet), first alpine-style ascent of North Face

1975: Summited Huayna Potisi (20,000 feet), Bolivia, first ascent of West Face (alpine-style)

1976: Summited Nanda Devi (25,645 feet), India, first ascent of North Face/Ridge

1977: Summited Trango Tower (20,250 feet), Pakistan Karakoram, first ascent

1978: Two-man alpine-style attempt on Jannu North Face, Nepal

Himalaya
1978: Summited K2 (28,250 feet), Pakistan Karakoram, first ascent of Northeast Ridge
1978: Received the Inland Empire Sportswriters & Broadcasters Certificate of Excellence for K2
1978: Received the Greater Spokane Sports Association Contribution to the Inland Empire Sports Program Award
1979: Summited Gaurishankar (23,440 feet), Nepal Himalaya, first ascent
1979: Summited Uli Biaho Tower (20,000 feet), Pakistan Karakoram, first ascent
1980: Summited Makalu (27,790 feet), world's fifth highest, Nepal Himalaya, second ascent of West Ridge
1982: Summited Cholatse (22,128 feet), Nepal Himalaya, first ascent done alpine-style
1982: My son, Jess, was born
1983: Received the first annual Robert and Miriam Underhill Award for Outstanding Mountaineering Achievement from the American Alpine Club
1984: Aconcagua (22,835 feet)
1984: Mount Everest, reached 28,000 feet from the north without bottled oxygen
1984: Received City of Spokane World Class Achievement Award
1985: Mount Kangchenjunga, reached 26,000 feet on the North Face
1987: *Nanda Devi: The Tragic Expedition* published
1989: Summited Tawoche (21,535 feet), Nepal Himalaya, alpine-style in winter, first ascent of Northeast Face
1989: My daughter, Jordan, was born
1990: Attempt on Menlungste (23,560 feet), Tibet Himalaya
1990: Received Honorary Membership, Spokane Mountaineers
1991: *Last Days* published
1991: Summited Denali (20,320 feet)
1992: Received Washington State University Alumni Association's Alumni Achievement Award
1993: Everest attempt via North Col route with Jim Wickwire
1995: Summited Mt. Sarmiento, Tierra del Fuego, first ascent west peak
1995: Elected Spokane County Commissioner
1997: Stok Kangri, Indian Himalaya; guide

THE MOUNTAINEERS, founded in 1906, is a nonprofit outdoor activity and conservation club, whose mission is "to explore, study, preserve, and enjoy the natural beauty of the outdoors...." Based in Seattle, Washington, the club is now the third-largest such organization in the United States, with 15,000 members and five branches throughout Washington State.

The Mountaineers sponsors both classes and year-round outdoor activities in the Pacific Northwest, which include hiking, mountain climbing, ski-touring, snowshoeing, bicycling, camping, kayaking and canoeing, nature study, sailing, and adventure travel. The club's conservation division supports environmental causes through educational activities, sponsoring legislation, and presenting informational programs. All club activities are led by skilled, experienced volunteers, who are dedicated to promoting safe and responsible enjoyment and preservation of the outdoors.

The Mountaineers Books, an active, nonprofit publishing program of the club, produces guidebooks, instructional texts, historical works, natural history guides, and works on environmental conservation. All books produced by The Mountaineers are aimed at fulfilling the club's mission.

If you would like to participate in these organized outdoor activities or the club's programs, consider a membership in The Mountaineers. For information and an application, write or call The Mountaineers, Club Headquarters, 300 Third Avenue West, Seattle, Washington 98119; (206) 284-6310.

Send or call for our catalog of more than 300 outdoor books:
The Mountaineers Books
1001 SW Klickitat Way, Suite 201
Seattle, WA 98134
1-800-553-4453